Organic AI

Bruno Maisonnier is one of the most distinctive figures in the French tech startup ecosystem. He is the founder of Aldebaran Robotics, the famous company behind the companion robots NAO and Pepper, which became the world leader in humanoid robots at its peak. He later co-founded about fifteen French deep-tech startups, spanning fields from space to surgical robotics, industrial 3D printing, heads-up display technology, and healthcare. His hallmark lies at the intersection of scientifically grounded concepts, a non-academic, almost artisanal approach to execution, and an immense technological ambition, directly targeting the goal without wasting time on intermediate steps. Having lived in various countries across Europe, Latin America, and Asia, he chose Paris as the location to create AnotherBrain, a company focused on producing electronic chips that function like the brain, in order to finally achieve truly intelligent Artificial Intelligence that is portable, energy-efficient, and optimized for minimal data consumption. A general AI inspired by nature—an "Organic AI."

First published in French under the title:
Organic AI. Comment les stratégies de la nature peuvent révolutionner l'intelligence artificielle, Hermann, 2024.

The publisher thanks Nathalia Barbosa for her contribution to the creation of the cover design.

www.editions-hermann.fr

ISBN print: 979 1 0370 4514 0

ISBN ebook: 979 1 0370 4416 7

Bruno Maisonnier

ORGANIC AI

How nature's principles can transform artificial intelligence

Translated from the French by Laurie Hurwitz

hermann

Depuis 1876

Introduction

In this book, we will talk about artificial intelligence, the famous AI, but also about real intelligence. We have all come to realize that AI is now a part of our lives, and for the long term. That it is at the heart of our smartphones, our businesses, our healthcare, our industries, our cars, and that it will gradually be everywhere.

But we've also realized that AIs, Deep Learning, LLMs, and other ChatGPTs need enormous amounts of data to function, often your data and ours. And that their carbon footprint is monstrous: from data centers to connected devices, the environmental cost of digital technology, including AI, is rising sharply. It already accounts for between 3 and 4% of global greenhouse gas emissions—on par with or even greater than aviation—and it is increasing rapidly.

We have also come to realize that there is no true intelligence in AI, only massive, raw calculations, which explains its carbon footprint. Of course, we don't really care whether it's intelligent or not, as long as AIs provide us with solutions—for example, detecting cancers at very early stages. And it would matter little to us if it weren't for the questions of carbon footprint and the enormous amounts of data needed, which, aside from privacy and cost issues, limit AI applications to fields where this data is accessible… AI must overcome these two obstacles. But how?

It turns out that we are surrounded by natural kinds of intelligence—those of humans, mammals, and other animals—far more powerful, capable of offering even more solutions, without the side effects of artificial intelligence. Why not draw inspiration from them to create AI that is much more energy- and data-efficient? Truly intelligent AI? "Organic AI."

Well, most of your interlocutors will answer that it's simply because we don't really know what intelligence is, or how it works. Because the human brain "is the most complex object in the known universe," as American neuroscientist Christof Koch wrote.

But what if we knew more than we think? And what if enough knowledge was available to achieve this goal? This is what a number of us believe, and what I will present to you in this book. What we know about how intelligence works, how to model it, and how to translate it into AI. So, into Organic AI.

1

Nature's simplex strategies

Imagine you're a bee. Around you, the hive is humming as it always does at the beginning of spring, overcrowded by the wave of births that came with the last solstice, since the winter days began to lengthen and gave the queen the signal to start laying again. The hive population has increased dramatically, consuming honey reserves at an accelerated rate. Will they last until the spring flowering, until the new harvest? Enough is enough: the colony decides to swarm, setting off in search of a new home. A new beginning. One more. The queen, now lighter and ready for flight, leaves the hive. She clings to a nearby branch, surrounded and protected by ten thousand worker bees until the scout bees return to announce they've found a new home. A new beginning, together.

But where, then, to build this new hive? How to choose the ideal cavity, not too small to be able to store enough honey to get through the next winter, but not too large, either, to exhaust the bees building oversized wax combs; with a well exposed opening to protect against the cold, and placed high enough to escape honey predators—but not too high to avoid the birds that prey on the bees… What a challenge!

No individual bee has the cognitive abilities to judge the "quality" of a nest cavity, let alone to compare two of them, or to discuss with the others the relative merits of the sites that each of them has found. And yet, within a radius of seven kilometers, the bees systematically make the best possible choice. Amazing!

Nevertheless, the following winter will be fatal for most new swarms. In 75% of cases, the best site turns out to be inadequate. The selection pressure is enormous. But thanks to their ability to act in a synergistic way, bees do their best and preserve their species[1]: the whole is greater than the sum of its parts.

More specifically, thanks to each individual performing a multitude of actions, not really coordinated in the way one might imagine, without a directive, leader, project manager, or queen giving orders or directions, each bee autonomously performing its tasks, the solution to the problem emerges. These tasks are automatic, almost mechanical, and don't require "intelligence"; they are not performed with the goal of solving a problem or addressing a specific point, but simply triggered by the situation each bee finds itself in at a given moment, which may have been the result of the actions of others, but not necessarily.

To illustrate: when the swarm has stabilized, clinging to its branch, the youngest bees in the center surrounding the queen and the oldest ones on top, the "dance of the old bees" begins: bees from the surface

---

1. See Thomas D. Seeley, *Honeybee Democracy* (Princeton: Princeton University Press, 2010).

of the swarm, among the few hundred older bees, decide to explore the surroundings, going in random directions to search for a cavity. They roughly assess what they find, each in their own way, and return to the swarm at their own pace. Along the way, it's the return to the swarm that justifies the exploration by the older bees: they know better than the young ones how to find the way back. More experience.

Once back on the surface of the swarm, they do their figure-eight dance: a few steps straight ahead, wiggling their behinds, then a half-circle to the left to return to the starting point, then a few more steps straight ahead, wiggling, and a half-circle to the right to return to the starting point. A circle and its diagonal. The angle between the vertical and the diagonal indicates the direction of the cavity relative to the sun, and the frequency of the wiggles indicates the distance.

They dance for longer if they've positively evaluated the location. Then they return, come back, do their choreography again, but for a shorter time, and so on, until they only perform one loop upon returning; then they stop and rest. They return to being "old wanderers" on the surface of the swarm.

That's all the explorers do. Without realizing that other old wanderers see them doing their dance, follow them for a loop or two, learning where the spot they have found is, and then go to explore it themselves. And return. And dance. Recruiting other explorers in the process.

Of course, other melliferous Indiana Joneses have identified other places, and through their dances, more or less long, they will also recruit more or fewer followers. Some bees will dance for different sites. But the mechanism of reducing the dance time with each return leads more and more bees to focus on the best site. Eventually, most of the bees will be dancing for the same place. The choice of the best site for the swarm has been made.

But how do the bees, who don't have an overview or the ability to discuss, inform each other and decide that they have a solution within reach of their wings?

Always through simple mechanisms: when the number of bees on the candidate site exceeds a threshold (about twenty individuals), the migration is triggered. The explorers return to the swarm, cross it from one side to the other, wriggling frantically, signaling to all that it's time to leave; the swarm disbands and takes off at low altitude. Low altitude because the explorers, the ones who know where to go, fly to higher altitudes to be visible to all, guiding the swarm like stars guiding the wise men.

But beware! These simple yet incredibly effective behaviors are not infallible: a careful reader will have noticed that the presence of more than twenty bees on a site doesn't guarantee it's THE best site; this number is an indicator of significant interest in a site, but another site could present an interest just as great (not much greater, or it would have already been selected). In fact, it sometimes happens—fortunately rarely—that at the swarm's starting signal, it splits in two, each part heading for a different place… This either means certain death or the return, disappointed, to the mother hive.

It's also worth noting that the evaluation of a site by a bee doesn't need to be precise, because the overall evaluation resulting from the process is the average of many evaluations by different bees, at different times. A precise result can emerge from many rough assessments. That's powerful!

*

I've illustrated two simple, mechanical behaviors that don't require intelligence and contribute to swarming. To fully understand how the explorers evaluate the quality of a site, it would be necessary to add a few more behaviors, and others still—equally mechanical and simplistic—but my purpose here is not to describe the operational methods of bees. Thomas D. Seeley's excellent book does a much better job than I ever could.

What I want to illustrate is how a set of simple agents, all identical, equipped with a range of mechanical behaviors like "if I'm in this situation, then I trigger this behavior," can demonstrate sophisticated decision-making within ecological constraints, without any of the agents being equipped with sufficient cognitive capacity.

It's not even necessary for the bees to know that they are searching for a new home. They only need to have the right range of behaviors, which have been fine-tuned by nature over a few hundred million years of evolution.

Let me be clear: I'm not diminishing bees in any way! I have great admiration for their capabilities. But that's no reason to fantasize about them or attribute human characteristics to them. On the contrary, it's exactly as they are that fascinates me, not by anthropomorphizing them.

It's common, in fact, to attribute collective intelligence to bees, as well as to other social insects. But there's no evidence of that—only the combination of a set of mechanical automata, even though they're alive, resulting in a process that can be described as intelligent. This raises questions about the very nature of intelligence.

A hive, an ant colony, or a school of fish can be called "multi-agent systems" (MAS), and the book that follows argues that our intelligence works in the same way. The "agents" in our brain are parts of our cortex, the cortical micro-columns, which gather neurons capable of performing a portion of the process of intelligence, a portion that is analyzable and describable. The full process of intelligence only emerges when these portions combine and interact dynamically. These cortical micro-columns, just like the bees in a colony, perform simple but interconnected tasks. Each micro-column, by connecting to others, participates in a broader network where processes of intelligence emerge from their dynamic interaction.

Before delving into the main topic of this book—the possibility of inventing a new AI that more closely resembles the actual functioning of our brain—I'd like to mention a few other natural multi-agent systems and clarify the major traits of nature's simplex strategies—the very strategies that could allow us to radically transform the nature of current AIs.

*

Imagine you're an acacia tree. Despite your thorns, your leaves are exposed to the robust tongue of giraffes, for whom your foliage is a prized delicacy, and this long-necked species is the only one in the African savanna that can enjoy it.

But you don't just stand there and take it. As soon as the ruminant's lips and teeth begin to nibble at you, you trigger a chemical response that quickly raises the level of toxins in your leaves.

Within minutes, the taste becomes unpleasant. You narrowly avoid a leafy demise, and the giraffe moves away and goes after your neighbors. Or at least, that's how one might imagine the next events. But your defense system doesn't stop there.

Having been attacked, you simultaneously release ethylene, a warning gas that informs all the nearby acacias of the danger. And they trigger the same reaction as you, even though they haven't been bitten at all. The giraffes know this well, often moving a hundred meters away before attacking one of your fellow acacias; or they will move upwind to attack the trees that haven't been alerted by your scent signal.

Among acacias, the whole is greater than the sum of its parts. They all have a vested interest in grouping together in groves, allowing them to better protect each other. Communicating, defending with active strategies… it's fascinating!

The forest as a whole, as we learn from the fascinating book by Peter Wohlleben[2] from which this example is taken, is a "multi-agent system," a collective in which communication, reaction, and

2. Peter Wohlleben, *The Hidden Life of Trees: What They Feel, How They Communicate—Discoveries from A Secret World* (Vancouver: Greystone Books, 2016).

adaptation occur constantly. The boundary between the plant world and the world of intelligence may be blurrier than we think. In fact, neuroscientists often represent the brain as a forest made up of special trees: the neurons, with their trunks—the axons—and their countless mutual connections—the synapses.

Now, you are a termite. You measure just a few millimeters in length and are even more primitive and rudimentary than ants and bees. And yet, by working together with 50,000 others, you manage to build termite mounds several meters high, with air conditioning—inside, it can be up to 12°C cooler than outside, never exceeding 28°C even when it's 40°C outdoors, and of course, it consumes no energy. The airflow is controlled, as well as the humidity. When I say "controlled," I don't mean fluctuating around an approximate average value: certain rooms where eggs are stored are warmer and drier, those where pieces of leaves are stored (on which fungi grow that the termites feed on) are warmer and more humid, while the waste storage areas are cooler… It's the work of an architect or engineer! And yet, no termite has the cognitive ability to understand that it's building a termite mound, let alone plan its actions for a specific outcome.

When European explorers started the photographic archiving of Africa in the nineteenth century, ethnographic pictures showing the continent's inhabitants next to the elegant architectural forms you built with your colony members began to multiply. You quickly earned the nickname "white ants." Your "cathedrals" left a lasting impression on the imagination of engineers and may have even inspired the vertical architecture of the following century.

Termites, like bees or ants, are social insects—or more precisely, "eusocial." The difference is important: cockroaches, for example, are social insects living in large colonies of identical insects, whose collective behaviors remain the sum of individual behaviors; eusocial insects, on the other hand, have a higher social organization, with cooperation in raising young generations that overlap, allowing for continuity and transmission, as well as division of labor by age and caste. This leads to individual behaviors based on the results of others and the emergence of collective behaviors.

The whole is greater than the sum of the parts. Despite having a tiny brain, termites use the few neurons that populate their long, thin bodies to produce effects they would be incapable of achieving on their own.

Naturalists have formalized the behavioral code of termites, and computer scientists have done the same for the worker ants in their colonies. They have succeeded in demonstrating that, with a limited set of rules and a few basic behaviors programmed into each insect, the colony members develop these spectacular architectures, which could never have emerged from their tiny, isolated brains[3].

---

3. See Pierre Paul Grassé's work in three volumes, *Termitologia: anatomie, physiologie, biologie, systématique des termites* (Termitologia: anatomy, physiology, biology and systematics of termites) (Paris, New York: Elsevier Masson, 1982-1984).

Termites do like all species. They use natural mechanisms to invent original solutions to the challenges posed by their environment. The result is a sophisticated system that meets all the challenges faced by a social group: reproduction, cooperation, economy, stability, and even ecology[4].

When reduced to their elementary traits, one might be tempted to see the constitution of termites as a simple mechanism. But at a very advanced degree, it accounts for the complexity of the world they face. In fact, the constitution of termites isn't simple at all. One might more accurately call it an example of "simplexity."

This was already the case with the selection of swarm sites by bees, another example of simplexity, where seemingly complex choices emerge from simple rules. Similarly, in human cognitive systems, complex decisions can emerge from simple, well-orchestrated processes.

Simplexity is to simplicity what complexity is to "complicated." It is an essential simplicity that comes from finding a different way to approach problems so that their resolution becomes easy. In science, one would say: a transposition of the problem into a space where the resolution becomes simpler.

The concept of simplexity was introduced in France by Alain Berthoz, a professor of neurophysiology at the Collège de France, during a seminar on movement. He later published a book of the same name, the introduction of which compares the

4. Éric Darrouzet, *Les Insectes sociaux* (Social insects) (Versailles: Quae, 2016).

properties of natural solutions with the increasing complexity of the environment in which we live. "Our brains are overwhelmed by the immense quantity of information required to live, act, and understand,"[5] he notes, before adding that the omnipresent reign of complexity provokes a reaction that is as natural as it is pernicious: an illusory quest for simplification, the disastrous consequences of which we know all too well.

The term simplexity, which Alain Berthoz borrows from English, literally means the opposite. Etymologically, that which is simplex is not something that presents itself in a flat manner, but something that is "folded, intertwoven" with something else. But with what? The complexity of the world itself.

Alain Berthoz's idea is that living organisms, confronted with an environment they perceive as complex, do not react in a simplistic manner. Instead, they reduce this complexity by shaping a perspective that suits them.

> "These solutions are indeed simplifying principles that reduce the number or the complexity of processes. They make it possible to rapidly analyze information or situations, taking into account past experience and anticipating the future—which helps to grasp intention—all the while respecting the complexity of reality. In my view, the ensemble of these solutions is simplexity. Simplex solutions are not just ways of reformulating or summarizing a problem. Put another way, they enable actions that are

5. Alain Berthoz, *Simplexity*. (New Haven: Yale University Press, 2012). Translated by Giselle Weiss from the French (*La Simplexité*. Paris: Odile Jacob, 2009), p. ix.

> more elegant, faster, and more efficient. They also give priority to the senses, even if it means making a detour."[6]

Transposing the problem into a space where its resolution becomes simple.

Throughout his book, Alain Berthoz enumerates the various mechanisms that allow for such solutions,

> "simplifying principles that reduce the number or the complexity of processes. They make it possible to rapidly analyze information or situations, taking into account past experience and anticipating the future—which helps to grasp intention—all the while respecting the complexity of reality."[7]

*

I have personally encountered this kind of mechanism, and it has greatly influenced me. In fact, there were several long periods in my life when I was "stuck" in cars or airplanes. First, a period of several years during which my teams were spread across three locations, between Lyon, Bourg-en-Bresse, and Mâcon. I had to frequently visit two of these sites in the same day, meaning two hours of highway driving each day. Then a period of expatriation in Poland for four years, which required round-trip flights between Wroclaw and Paris twice a week due to family obligations, in addition to local flights in Poland (ten to twelve hours of flying each week). And others, which meant that no week passed without at least one transcontinental flight. During these long

6. *Ibid.*, p. xi.
7. *Idem.*

periods, I had a lot of time to think, but little time to take action.

But gradually, this structured me and led me toward optimizing my achievements and simplifying them as much as possible, so I could focus on what mattered. I would think through each step of the process—how to approach the task to minimize the time needed for completion—and I visualized how I was going to do it—not generally, no, but in a very concrete and practical way—to ensure that, the day when I would finally have a bit of time to act, I would have all the tools, and know every step of the process.

We know well that, when it comes to execution, things never go as planned. There's always a missing piece or tool, and the phases always take longer than expected… I made it a habit to take all of that into account, to find ways to minimize the uncertainties, and by constantly thinking about it and turning the issue around in my head from every angle, I optimized my actions to be as efficient as possible. Pragmatism in execution, and essential gestures. This had an immense impact on my way of functioning.

We are in great need of simplexity. That's what I told myself when I discovered these original reflections, which immediately resonated with my experience as a robotics engineer who later moved on to studying artificial intelligence. For several years now, I have been trying to propose innovative solutions inspired by nature to solve the challenge of creating general artificial intelligence, capable of truly understanding its environment. A natural artificial intelligence, or, better yet, as I like to say, an

"Organic AI," in the sense of something rooted in biology and inspired by nature.

Before that, I concentrated for years on imagining the most elegant solutions to problems that, from the outside, seem trivial, but actually concern the stability of a robot, its ability to grasp objects, its contextual sense, and its capacity to perform gestures that seem natural. With my first company, Aldebaran Robotics, we succeeded enough in this field to make two of our creations famous: the Nao and Pepper robots. At each stage of my experience as an inventor, but also as a maker and polycraftsman, I had to rely on simplexity strategies at play in nature.

Among them, the principle of "modularity." A key strategy, which allows each complex cognitive or sensorimotor function to be separated into specialized modules that cooperate, offering an analogue of our division of labor in society.

This is a very powerful way to achieve a second principle, that of "speed," which allows both organisms and brains to play their role as living beings, constantly facing a changing present.

A third principle mentioned in the repertoire of simplex strategies is "vicariance" or "substitution": considering a plurality of possible paths to solve a single problem.

Here, we see the difference between simplicity and simplexity. During rush hour, in heavy traffic, taking a direct bus line from point A to point B is certainly the simplest solution, but it is far from the most effective. The most efficient solution is, for example, taking a commuter train and making a transfer somewhere—a detour that adds complexity, but an interesting complexity, which turns out to be a winning bet for the future. Or, on the contrary, the ability to take the bus if there are construction works or a breakdown on the train line.

Readers who refer to Chapter 3 of Alain Berthoz's book will discover other principles, equally stimulating, drawn from these ideas. What is essential for me is to emphasize that the demand for simplexity arises from the complexity we are immersed in. We live in a changing world, and to survive, we must be able to anticipate, decide wisely, and navigate through the accidents of time and the irregularities of space, in order to achieve the goals we set for ourselves.

In an era where the term AI is everywhere, and the challenge is precisely to develop an effective AI—meaning one that is energy-efficient and in touch with the world—it seems to me that a detour through what we know about natural simplexity and the way our own brain operates can be quite enlightening.

It's important to know that the brain, which is still infinitely superior to existing artificial intelligences, can understand and learn with a regular consumption of just 20 watts—roughly the energy of a light bulb or an LED screen in standby mode. And even more strikingly, most of this energy consumption isn't tied to cognition, but rather to bodily management. For cognition itself, we're probably talking about only 19% of the total—just 4 to 5 watts!

Since my adolescence, I have been passionately interested in Darwin's theory of evolution. Some knowledge has evolved, especially with the discovery of the importance of epigenetics, but the core principle has remained largely the same. From this, I've gained the profound conviction that nature works gradually, and has a remarkable capacity for optimization.

Above all, this is what nature does: optimize, again and again. It doesn't always invent amazing things. Nature didn't invent the wheel, for example. But it tackles problems to be solved in a subtly clever way—finding solutions that are simple, such as by placing any problem in an appropriate frame of reference that leads to an answer.

It seems to me that this is what we are invited to do if we want to create meaningful inventions for the future. Once we have established the major guiding ideas and unifying frameworks, we need to be incredibly skillful and tireless in pursuing gradual optimization—an ongoing, progressive improvement of our discoveries, in a way that is not simplistic, but simplex.

In the chapters that follow, I will delve into the heart of our brain. We often hear that it is very complex; yet this complexity generates a certain opacity that deserves to be questioned. We're told it's so complex that it's not worth the effort to try to understand it, that it somehow eliminates the very idea of trying… So, I'll attempt to take stock of what we know about it by flipping the perspective. What is the brain? How does it work? Based on which mechanisms—not simple, but simplexes? The brain, through mechanisms like lateral inhibition and synaptic plasticity, perfectly illustrates this simplexity by constantly optimizing information processing while minimizing energy consumption. It's a true machine of simplexity, and we have much to learn from it.

I'll then explore the fascinating concept of "tactical patterns". A way of reading the world that allows us to map analogies between the most everyday situations and the most speculative challenges. If cognition essentially involves recognizing such patterns, analyzing them, and labeling them, it's crucial to understand how identifying them helps us survive, and at which levels of reality we should look for them.

I'll then move on to the foundations of a model for creating natural-type artificial intelligences, which I call Organic AI. This will be a different kind of AI—autonomous, genuinely intelligent, creative, more effective and more energy-efficient than those currently being produced—mostly by American and Chinese industries, although France, as an agile follower, has some advantages that could help it stay in the race; but the strategy of hunting in the giants' playground, trying to do what they do with a hundred times fewer resources, is still worth questioning.

This book will conclude with an exercise in foresight. How will organic AIs change the world? What new role will they carve out for humans? In this context, I will revisit a question that particularly interests me: the implications of these innovations for the future of humanoid robotics.

2

The Brain, a machine of simplicity

To continue, let's transport ourselves to the Amazon. In the heart of the rainforest beneath the thick canopy of giants, there's deep darkness. Their energy comes from the sun. They capture every ray that penetrates, both for themselves—for photosynthesis—and to block out as much competition as possible. They have their "young" around them, and they need to nurture them. They reserve a less crowded space to help them grow, and they prepare a floor via their blanket of needles or leaves, creating an acidic soil for some species, alkaline for others, or by using various chemical additives to the soil, often with the help of their symbiotic fungi. It's vital to prepare conditions that are unfavorable to competing species but favorable to their own descendants.

And then, from time to time, disaster strikes: one of the giants falls, creating a gap of sunlight in the dark canopy. It's the start of a frenzied race to see who will seize the vacant spot, climb the fastest, and spread its branches to capture the sun's energy at the expense of other contenders. It's a veritable competition, with the starting signal coming at any moment, that will secure for the winner decades of prime exposure, the transmission of its genes, and a competitive advantage. There's a lot at stake. You must be prepared, have built up enough reserves, and have an appropriate strategy. It's a jungle out there.

But there are also bandits: the strangler fig doesn't wait for a venerable tree to fall—it orchestrates the collapse. As a young vine, it wraps itself around the adult trees, climbing higher as it thickens... This sneaky intruder strengthens its grip, tightening it, to the point of strangling and eventually killing the giant tree. By this point, the fig is already large enough to support itself, and monopolize the sunlight. It's a veritable hold-up.

Competitions, battles, strategies, nurseries, terraforming, and even communication and reactions to attackers—one could list many other behaviors of trees. Isn't there intelligence in that? But all of this happens at the slow pace of trees; the rhythm is measured not in seconds, minutes, or hours, nor even weeks or months, but in decades, even centuries. A rhythm that falls outside our own operational frequencies, and therefore something we cannot intuitively grasp.

We might imagine reducing tree behaviors to purely mechanical "action-reaction" systems, genetically encoded... But admit it, the line between that and *truly intelligent* systems is hard to draw, isn't it?

1. What is intelligence?

As a first point of attack, let's dive into what we know about the structure and function of the "cognitive brain of mammals."

To start, this odd term refers to the part of the brain responsible for managing most cognitive functions, so, roughly speaking, intelligence; and it doesn't just refer to the human brain, but to the various natural brains whose structure and functioning are similar.

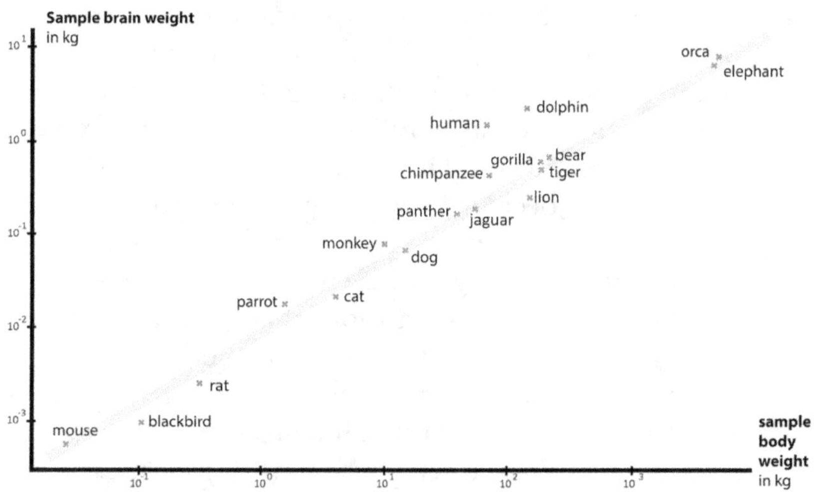

Fig. 1: Relation between brain weight and body weight for various animals and humans. Humans stand out, along with dolphins and apes.

Of course, the intelligence of animals—monkeys, dogs, pigs, or rats—doesn't match that of humans. Yet, humans don't have the largest brains (orcas and whales do), or even the most extensive cortex (dolphins); the differentiation between human intelligence and animal intelligence can be understood by looking at small differences in the structure of the cortex. Nevertheless, the way it functions is similar to that of other mammals. That's why I often prefer to talk about natural brains and intelligence, rather than human brain and intelligence. But for simplicity, I will use both terms interchangeably. Interestingly, birds, which have a different cortex than mammals, follow the same size ratio rule.

When I refer to the part of the brain responsible for most cognitive functions, I'm of course talking about the cortex. I can already hear the objections from those who will say "hippocampus," "cerebellum," "amygdala," and all the other brain regions necessary for proper functioning. Of course, the many neuroscientists working on these other parts do not accept limiting intelligence functions to the cortex alone, because everything in the brain is so interconnected. However, my aim here is not to create a human being—or even a brain—since the human brain does much more than just manage intelligence (including managing the body's infrastructure, immunity, emotions, stability, etc.), but to solely to get closer to that intelligence.

Even for "pure" intelligence, if that even means anything, the thalamus and hippocampus are necessary, but not to understand the core functioning of intelligence. I will deliberately focus on the cortex, which is responsible for most cognitive functions, because intelligence can be understood by focusing on the cortex.

Jeff Hawkins, in his book *On Intelligence*, points out the vast number of publications on the brain, focusing on specific aspects, which seem to scatter in every direction, and giving the impression of great confusion about the knowledge surrounding it. For example, if you're interested in dopamine, a neurotransmitter, you'll find about 160,000 publications on the subject. It's difficult to get a clear overview… Anyone interested in the brain and natural intelligence today might feel as though they're in the same situation as scientists in the eighteenth and nineteenth centuries when faced with contagious diseases. Back then, there was a proliferation of diseases, and for each one, medicine tried treatments and prevention strategies that were not very effective without understanding the underlying phenomena. It wasn't until the discovery of the bacterial origins of these diseases in the second half of the nineteenth century (Filippo Pacini for cholera, Casimir Davaine for anthrax, then the multiplication of coherent discoveries). Then, a marvelous solution emerged: their common treatment through antibiotics. Once the general framework of contagious diseases was understood, a significant portion of humanity's suffering was alleviated. It "only" took finding the right perspective.

We are currently at this stage regarding understanding how the brain works, and it's not a lack of data that hinders us, but rather a lack of a unifying and simplifying framework. Just as the periodic table revolutionized chemistry or the double helix transformed biology, we need a framework that simplifies, but also generates models that can provide intelligent solutions.

Simplifying, because it's by reducing things to their essentials, at the heart of processes stripped of all refinements and complexities, that we can truly understand and replicate them. We can always refine our understanding later. This is the key to understanding the functioning of intelligence at its core.

This is exactly what Jeff Hawkins is doing with his company, Numenta, a private research lab in California.[1] Or Yves Burnod, a neuroscientist and research director at CNRS and Inserm, who has done groundbreaking work in brain mapping alongside his wife, Nikki,[2] as well as powerful meta-analyses on the brain.

I owe much to the scientists who have dedicated decades to uncovering the mysteries of the brain, but my particular debt is to those pioneers of complexity reduction.

2. THE HEART OF COGNITIVE BRAIN: THE CORTEX AND ITS NEURONS

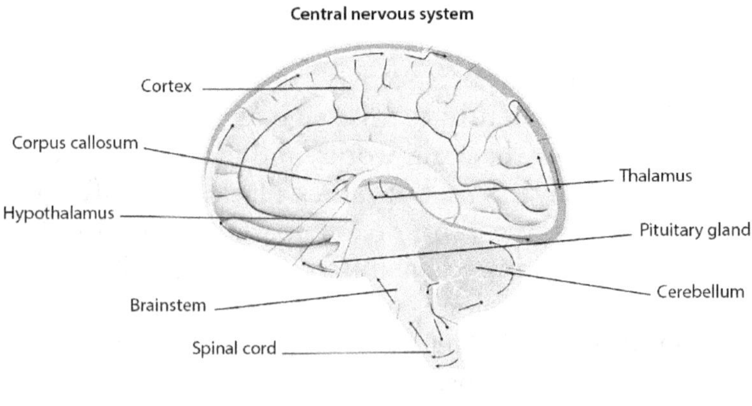

Fig. 2: Structure of the brain.

1. Jeff Hawkins, *A Thousand Brains: A New Theory of Intelligence* (New York: Basic Books, 2021).

2. Yves and Nikki Burnod, *The Panoramic Brain. A panorama of brain resources to boost education and address the Web and AI challenges* (self-published, 2024).

Let's return to the structure of the brain.

Its largest part consists of two hemispheres, covered with convolutions and some large separating grooves. Just beneath, or wrapped inside, are several subcortical organoids (hippocampus, cerebellum, amygdala, hypothalamus…), and a large whitish cord extends downward from it—the spinal cord.

Of course, all these elements are essential for the functioning of the brain and the human body, but when it comes to cognitive functions and intelligence, it is primarily the hemispheres that are in charge. More precisely, the gray matter layer that we find when we slice the hemispheres in half horizontally—a thin layer a few millimeters thick that follows the contour of the hemispheres and traces all their grooves: the cortex. It's as if the cortex were a kind of waxed cloth, 2 millimeters thick, with the consistency of a very soft fabric like cotton or silk, and a surface area of about one-third of a square meter, crumpled to fit into the skull, and whose internal space is filled with connections between the different parts of its surface (the white matter). See Figure 4.

A remarkable and totally structuring fact for everything that follows is that this piece of waxed cloth, once unfolded, is of very high homogeneity. There are no physical boundaries, no color or texture changes, even at the microscopic level. We know, of course, that there are zones with different roles, because localized injuries in specific parts of the cortex cause certain functions to be lost but not others. MRIs that record brain activity have made significant progress in mapping these hemispheres and have created actual atlases of all the zones of the cortex.[3] But no physical demarcation is observed between these areas in the cortex, which seems to be *structured functionally* rather than physically.

Of course, the cortex is filled with the famous cells of intelligence that are the neurons. The human brain contains just under a hundred billion of them, around 86 billion to be precise, of which the cortex holds just under 20%. And yes, as surprising as it may seem, the majority of our neurons serve purposes other than intelligence. Nevertheless, the cortex remains very densely populated with 16 billion neurons, whose cell bodies are all contained within this thin 2-millimeter-thick layer of waxed cloth.

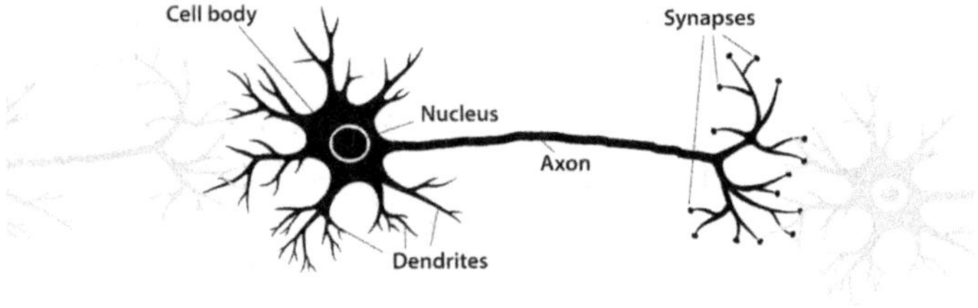

Fig. 3: Structure of a neuron.

Cell bodies? Each neuron consists of three major parts. First, the cell body itself, that somewhat fleshy part of the neuron, which houses all the cellular machinery necessary for its functioning, such as the nucleus containing DNA, the mitochondria for energy, ribosomes for protein synthesis, and other components that don't need to be detailed here. Next,

3. See for example T.B. Leergaard and J.G. Bjaalie, "Atlas-Based Data Integration for Mapping the Connections and Architecture of the Brain," *Science*, November 3, 2022.

the dendritic tree, a branching structure of filaments that extend from the neuron's body, the dendrites, and essentially serve as receptors for information or impulses coming from other neurons. This is where the neuron receives and begins processing information. Finally, a long filament called the axon extends from the cell body, sometimes traveling long distances, before dividing into multiple branches that connect to the dendrites of other neurons. It is through this path that information exits the neuron.

The connection between an axonal terminal of one neuron and a dendrite of another occurs via synapses. These are small buttons filled with chemical molecules—neurotransmitters, such as glutamate—that are released into the space between neurons when the upstream part of a synapse is activated; these molecules activate the downstream part of the synapse on the other neuron, by binding to receptor molecules such as the glutamate receptor, thus stimulating the receiving dendrite and transmitting the information to the next neuron.

The cell bodies of neurons and their dendritic trees are located in the cortex, and most of the axons and their branches land there, which is where the synapses are.

Each neuron has up to 10,000 synapses for large pyramidal neurons, meaning 10,000 connections with other neurons. However, these connections are often made with the same neuron since, on average, one neuron is connected to another by a hundred synapses. This gives the same coding power as a 100-bit word in computing.

Thus, 16 billion neurons, each connected to about a hundred others via 10,000 synapses, form the cortex... Hello, complexity! How do we navigate through this gigantic plate of spaghetti?

In the following pages, I will focus on decisive neurophysiological discoveries from the twentieth century, which revolutionized our understanding of the arrangement of neurons in the cortex, and allow us to sketch a much clearer and more useful map of the operations of intelligence.

3. MICROCOLUMNS

In the 1980s, when the great homogeneity of the cortical surface, very uniform, was noticed, rather than exploring the consequences of this uniformity, anatomists, convinced that speech, vision, and hearing were fundamentally different, focused on the subtle differences "that were **necessarily** required" between the areas of the cortex to treat these senses in a distinct manner. And upon examining them closely, they did indeed find them.

That's when Vernon Benjamin Mountcastle, a neuroscientist at Johns Hopkins University, chose to take the opposite approach: since the cortical surface is so homogeneous, all its regions might perform the same basic operations, and the cortex could be using the same mechanisms 'everywhere.'[4]

4. Vernon B. Mountcastle, "An organizing principle for cerebral function: the unit module and the distributed system," in *The Mindful Brain. Cortical Organization and a Selective Theory of Brain Function* (Cambridge: MIT Press, 1978).

His work was groundbreaking and became a foundational hypothesis in neuroscience. However, this perspective remained largely overlooked in the development of AI, where different paradigms took precedence.

Upon examining the cortex more closely, and even very closely, it became evident that the neurons are not arranged randomly, as if it were simply a gigantic network of neurons. Not at all. In fact, they are grouped into small packets of approximately 110 neurons, forming columns that are 2 millimeters long and about 50 μ in diameter: these structures, visible across the entire waxed cloth of the cortex, were named by Mountcastle as "cortical columns," which a later discovery invites us to refer to more specifically, at this basic level, as micro-columns (or micro-columns).

The major contribution of these cortical columns is that their neurons have a very particular connection architecture, which has become increasingly refined throughout evolution. As if one neuron were replaced by a super-neuron made of 110 different neurons communicating very closely with each other.

Two neurons communicating with each other have a limited exchange capacity, with one axon per neuron, much like two people exchanging only emojis, whereas 110 neurons per column allow for messages to be exchanged on 110 axons in parallel.

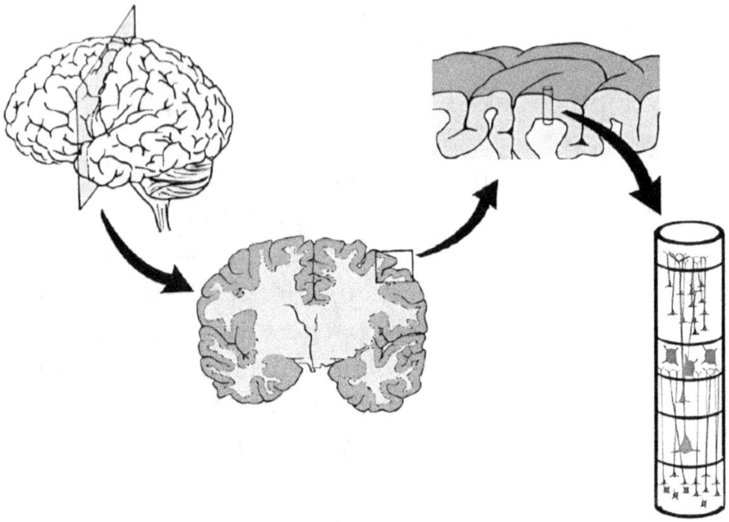

Fig. 4: The cortex is a homogeneous surface paved with identical micro-columns.

The neurons here are of different types; the connection plan between them is becoming well known; and what is remarkable is that the entire cortex is paved with these cortical columns, arranged side by side transversely, with nothing else in the cortex; but also that these micro-columns are all identical.

Not strictly identical, because their history, their "experience," will lead them to specialize, their synapses to multiply and grow, and their structure to change slightly; but essentially identical in their nature and functioning. This is what strengthens Mountcastle's argument.

The experience of sensory crossovers is a striking demonstration of this. At one point on this waxed cloth of the cortex, the optic nerve arrives: this zone of the cortex will process vision and become the primary visual area (V1). At another point, the auditory nerve arrives, and the cortex zone that receives these inputs will process hearing and become the primary auditory area (A1). To be more precise, the optic and auditory nerves don't directly arrive on the cortex but pass through relay stations, in the thalamus, from which they are projected to the visual and auditory cortices. However, as you will see next, this doesn't change the principles at play behind the sensory crossover experiments.

Experiments were conducted on embryos of ferrets and mice, in which the optic and auditory nerves were cut and crossed—directing visual input to the auditory cortex and auditory input to the visual cortex. As you might have guessed, the results were remarkable! The cortex adapted to process the new inputs. Can you imagine? Vision was processed by the part of the brain normally dedicated to hearing, and hearing by the visual cortex, and yet the animals were still able to process visual and auditory stimuli. What better proof that the brain, at its core, operates on the same basic principles across all its regions?

Inside these micro-columns, it is also found that the neuronal bodies are not evenly distributed, creating an alternating pattern of concentrations and gaps of neuronal bodies along a micro-column, which appear as darker and lighter spots. The side-by-side arrangement of these small columns across the entire surface of the cortex transforms their alternating light and dark spots into clear and dark bands, visible along the cortex's cross-section; thus, the cortex appears to have six layers, which leads us to another essential discovery.

4. The micro-column: a Swiss army knife of cognition

In the years that followed, building on the description by Vernon Mountcastle, David Hubel, and Torsten Wiesel of Harvard Medical School, the role of cortical micro-columns in the functioning of the visual cortex was further refined. They concluded that these micro-columns are a sort of *master algorithm*, a Swiss knife of cognition in the cortex that does everything and is responsible for all parts of cognition. Their work earned them the Nobel Prize in Medicine in 1981.[5]

Hubel and Wiesel pushed the research further, analyzing the functioning of the micro-columns and their six layers. They discovered that a combination of two layers analyzes the dynamics of the input signal on the column, thus reacting to the signal's evolution over time (analysis in d/dt); two other layers together perform a structural analysis of the signal (in d/dx this time), which analyzes the lateral variation of the signal between several contiguous micro-columns, and can provide information on ratios between inputs or the local orientation of the edges of a shape. Finally, a third analysis is made on the intensities of the incoming signals, i.e., the homogeneity of intensity between adjacent cortical columns, for example, to characterize color, luminance, or textures. Therefore, the micro-columns

---

5. David Hunter Hubel and Torsten Wiesel, *Brain and Visual Perception. The Story of a 25-year collaboration* (New York: Oxford University Press, 2004).

perform global, dynamic, and structural analyses of the signals they receive (GDS analyses).

The result of these analyses? The micro-columns are semantic translators. They receive various signals, which may come from other micro-columns or sensory sensors such as the retina for visual signals and the cochlea for auditory signals, always indirectly, through ganglia, and transform them into "words," into semantic labels. Careful, note that these are not "words" in the usual sense of vocabulary words, made up of letters of the alphabet, but rather just a label, a code that summarizes a bundle of detailed information. For example, it might translate a group of visual pixels into a code interpreted as a "line oriented at 45°" or a "yellow spot." We have moved up in abstraction by replacing a set of pixels with a meaningful label, a semantic label. Or it might translate another group of already identified and meaningful labels, such as "eye," "nose," "mouth," into a label of an even higher level of abstraction: "face." These labels, codes, or tags, which carry meaning and summarize a richer, more detailed reality, are like our "words." The micro-columns allow us to represent a sequence of pixels from the retina seen at the same time into a semantic label, such as "line oriented at 16°," "red-orange zone," "zone with a texture composed of more or less regular and more or less aligned dark parallel lines around 45°," "zone moving in such a direction, at such a speed," etc., each of the quoted phrases being a label I have illustrated here with a sentence for understanding what a semantic label is.

In the cortex, of course, nothing is so explicit; the labels are neurally encoded, if that even means anything. The column coding this sequence of pixels as a semantic label has enriched the description level, which I synthesize by the level of abstraction in understanding the input.

Other later columns might associate several oriented lines seen simultaneously that intersect in "angles," and others at an even higher level might combine several angles into a shape: "square," "triangle," "house," etc.

The two key elements here are temporal co-occurrence, meaning the simultaneous perception of signals, and their translation into semantic labels.

Temporal co-occurrence in the world results in the co-occurrence of signals on neurons, which is precisely what generates learning, since two simultaneous messages lead to the selective growth of synapses. Thanks to this co-occurrence, the semantic labels are gradually enriched. These simultaneously perceived semantic labels then serve as input to another micro-column, which labels these co-occurrences into a higher-level abstraction label: a column regularly receiving, simultaneously from other translating columns, labels such as "eye-eye-nose-mouth" could thus label a higher-level abstraction shape like "face." The qualification of "higher-level abstraction labels" is a metaphor illustrating that labels encompass increasingly larger and more complex realities, with richer descriptions as they integrate several columns through cascades of labeling, getting closer and closer to the co-occurrence sources of the surrounding world.

The important thing is to understand the great power of this construction, which appears so simple. We are at the heart of a mechanism of simplexity, which the Danish researcher Norbert Krüger referred to in his publication on the analysis of the macaque visual cortex as Deep Hierarchy (Jade was here—sorry, it's my daughter). Not only can all visible scenes be apprehended through a chain of GDS analyses, but once the input signals are translated into semantic labels, i.e., into "words," the system becomes agnostic to the type of initial data, whether it comes from the skin or the cochlea; it can also be generalized to apply to other realities beyond the visual reality: touch, hearing, etc.; this explains the homogeneity of the entire cortical structure, despite being dedicated to highly diverse tasks.

5. Cortical columns, or macro-columns

What inputs exactly do the micro-columns receive? The arrival of the optic nerves (or auditory nerves, or others) onto the cortex, indirectly through thalamic nodes, is genetically coded. They arrive at the same spot in the cortex for everyone. The micro-columns in this zone will, of course, process the elementary signals from the eyes and retinas. More precisely, the visual field of the retinas is projected onto an area of the cortex where the optic nerves arrive; each micro-column of these zones processes a small portion of the visual field. Each micro-column thus receives signals from a part of the retina and labels them, producing an output flow of labels that translate or describe the incoming visual flow into the eyes. However, the reverse is not true: each small portion of the visual field is not processed by one micro-column but by several adjacent ones, which analyze the same area of the receptive field. This cohort of micro-columns processing the same small portion of the receptive field is called a "cortical column" or "macro-column"; both terms coexist. Approximately 1,000 micro-columns (on average) make up a cortical column. These cortical column structures are not physically visible, not delimited, and their composition probably evolves over time—1,000 micro-columns per column seems to be an average with significant variation.

The general mechanism is as follows: cortical columns divide the receptive field to analyze—the visual field for sight, the tactile field for touch, etc.—with the micro-columns in each analyzing the same portion of the receptive field. They "laterally" feed off what neighboring columns have found and produce an output flow of labels that they send to higher-level cortical columns. What is true for primary cortical areas, which receive their signals from sensory sensors, is also true for other maps of higher abstraction levels, except for the type of receptive field analyzed by the columns, which is no longer an external field (vision, touch, smell...) but an "internal" field—for example, the flow of visual and auditory labels emanating from other cortical columns.

Finally, the last interesting and essential aspect is that these cortical columns evolve over time. They evolve because, by repeatedly receiving the same type of excitations, they learn them, learn to decode them, to see the essence of what they have in common, and what differentiates them from others that are similar to them. Thus, little by little, they evolve according to the signals they receive. They evolve over time, with some layers thickening due to the growth of their synapses, while others shrink, without completely changing structure or mechanism, of course, but they evolve. This specialization phenomenon justifies the interest of neurophysiologists in the small singularities of cortical areas, despite the overall homogeneity.

Mountcastle was right: there is indeed a powerful, unique algorithm at work throughout the cortex, a master algorithm of cognition. In 1978, Mountcastle explained that the cortex does everything with the same tool: the cortical micro-column. This is the philosopher's stone of intelligence, which has been dismissed by many as too simple—and it couldn't possibly be true because it was so simple. In reality, the solution is not simple but simplex. We will better understand what I mean when we think back to the social insects we encountered in the first chapter of this book.

Just think of the organizational marvels of an ant colony, the spectacular architectures of termites, or the selection of the best possible location by a swarm of bees; the determining feature is that of complex emergent phenomena resulting from the individual behaviors of "simple" agents, and which far exceed the cognitive capacities of each agent when taken in isolation.[6]

A bee, for example, has a tiny brain of 1 cubic millimeter, containing around 950,000 to 1 million neurons, most of which are responsible for managing

6. E. Darrouzet, *op. cit.*

the body's infrastructure. The portion dedicated to cognitive behaviors exceeds the 110 neurons of a micro-column but must be of an order of magnitude similar to that of a cortical column. One can draw a parallel between a cortical column and an insect from a eusocial insect colony like bees, ants, or termites.

The elegance of the solution is precisely the one that builds, with these very simple bricks, the properties of the phenomenon that transcends them, as researchers have shown in reconstructing the algorithm that enables ants to choose the optimal path between their colony and a food source. This decomposition was the subject of a important thesis by Italian computer scientist Marco Dorigo, *Ant System*[7]. Similar work was conducted in the 1950s by French zoologist Pierre-Paul Grassé on the construction of termite nests within the paradigm of "stigmergy[8]."

One can thus view the cortex as a particular multi-agent system in which the identical agents are cortical columns, some connected to our sensory receptors, others to other cortical columns, but processing all received signals in the same way. The model of cortical columns and the master algorithm proposes a simplifying, yet not simplistic, model that allows us to focus on intelligence as an effect of this simplex mechanism. Ultimately, all areas of the brain rely on this tool, the small cortical micro-column, and on its analyzable function. What makes it flexible is

7. Marco Dorigo, *Optimization, Learning and Natural Algorithms*. Ph.D. thesis, Politecnico di Milano, 1992.

8. "Stigmergy" ("stimulating work" from *stigma*, sting, and *ergon*, work) considers that agents do not guide their work, but are guided by it in positive feedback loops. In the case of termites, see P. Grassé, *op cit.*

what it is connected to. In other words, on the one hand, what information it is given to process, and on the other the circuits that its flow of labels feeds into. The mechanism is always the same. And that is why it is so powerful.

6. Details on the number of micro-columns and neurons

Determining the average number of neurons and synapses in *living* human brains is not a simple task. This explains the significant variability in published figures, and you may come across quite different values on this topic, just as I have. Regarding the count of cortical micro-columns, estimates range from 200 million to over 1 billion. The number of neurons per micro-column fluctuates between 80 and 110. As for the number of micro-columns per column, estimates vary widely, from 50 to 100, 400, or even 1,000.

More broadly, when it comes to neurons grouped within the cortex, estimates range from a lower bound of 15 or 16 billion to as many as 30 billion. Finally, the total surface area of this “waxed canvas” that is the cortex, directly linked to the total number of micro-columns that compose it, cannot yet be measured precisely and reliably, and there are few references to it in scientific literature. That said, precise figures are not essential for the purpose of this book. The goal is not to count the instruments with absolute accuracy but to understand the organization and mechanisms of intelligence.

7. The cortex has a geography

Now, let's take a step back to look at the organization of cortical columns and micro-columns. Cortical columns divide up different parts of the sensory fields they analyze, while the micro-columns within them work together to translate key, salient features from their small portion of the sensory field into a semantic label. The zone of the cortex that brings together all the columns responsible for analyzing the same sensory field is called a cortical map. Each cortical map thus corresponds to a complete sensory field that needs to be analyzed.

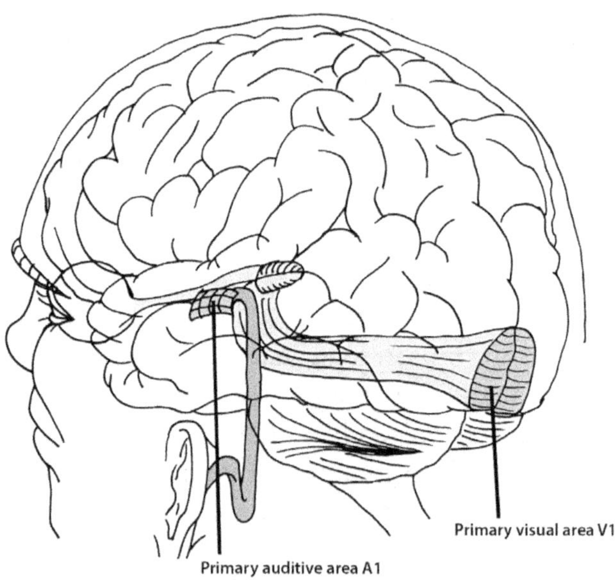

Fig. 5: Primary visual and auditory areas.

This organization is easy to grasp when looking at the zones of the cortex that receive direct sensory input. The visual field, or the sensory field of vision, is analyzed by the cortical columns that make up what we call the "visual area V1," a cortical map located where the optic nerves arrive in the brain. Similarly, there is an A1 map for auditory processing.

There is also a cortical map dedicated to bodily sensitivity, linking different areas of the body to corresponding regions of the cortex. Called the "Penfield homunculus," named after the Canadian neurosurgeon who published an atlas of sensory sensitivity in the brain in the 1940s, this map links different parts of the body according to their level of sensitivity to touch—that is, sensitivity to pressure, both external and internal—providing information about our body's state, posture, and the position of our organs and muscles. Penfield depicted this map in the form of a human figure, enlarging the areas that are more sensitive. More precisely, the areas requiring more micro-columns and cortical columns to process sensory information with greater precision. This has led to some highly expressive depictions.

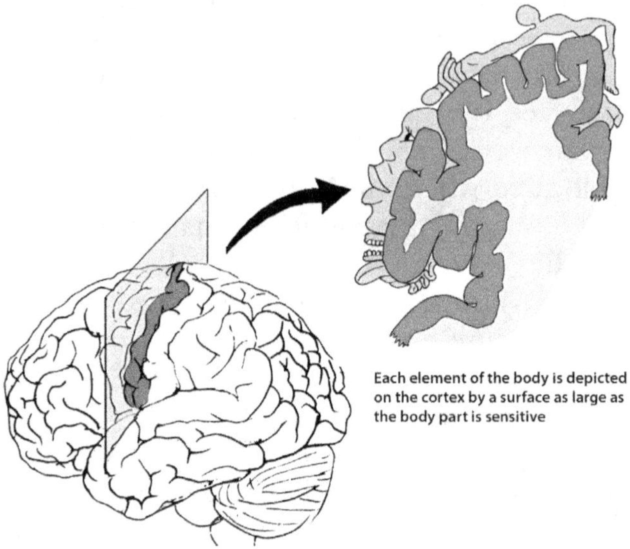

Fig. 6: Penfield's homunculus.

It should be noted by the way that what happens on the cortical map is a direct reflection of what happens in the body, slightly distorted according to sensitivities, but organized and structured in the same way. This property is called "topicality," and it is a characteristic of all cortical maps directly connected to the senses. Roger Tootell[9] demonstrated that the analysis of the visual area V1 in a macaque, to which a test pattern had been shown, revealed neuron activation exactly matching the pattern of the test. The V1 area is also topographically organized.

---

9. Roger B.H. Tootell, Eugene Switkes, Martin S. Silverman, and Susan L. Hamilton, "Functional Anatomy of Macaque Striate Cortex: II. Retinotopic Organization," *Journal of Neuroscience* 8, no. 5 (May 1988): 1531-68, <https://doi.org/10.1523/JNEUROSCI.08-05-01531.1988>.

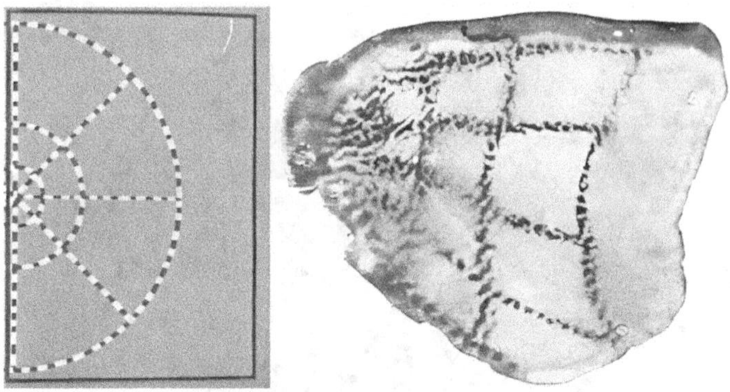

Fig. 7: Activation of the visual area in a macaque from a test pattern projected onto the eye.

On the other hand, the regions of the cortex dedicated to more abstract analyses are harder to identify. For example, the visual V2 map, which seems to only receive information from the V1 map, is not directly connected to the optic nerve. It processes the same receptive field, the visual field, but extends the work of the V1 area when images are complex, refining contours, especially those that are colored. There are still higher-level maps where the receptive field combines outputs from several other maps to label phenomena that are either more abstract or that involve multiple sensory modalities.

Thus, the cortex is paved with cortical maps that, each receiving input flows, translate them into labels with a slightly higher richness of description. Each map is equivalent to the others, functioning in the same way with its cortical columns distributing the analysis of its receptive field. There are an estimated 390 cortical maps in the human brain, with an *average* of 400 cortical columns per map.

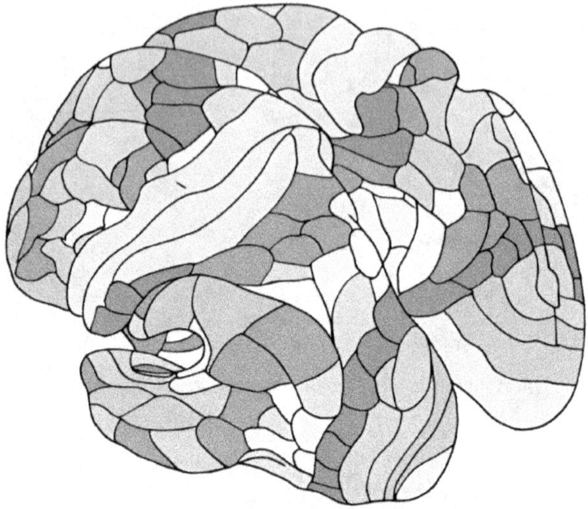

Fig. 8: Illustration of cortical maps.

What is intelligence? Now that we've seen how the cortex is organized into cortical maps, made up of cortical columns, which themselves group micro-columns, let's look at their mechanics.

Evolution, under the name brain, has developed a remarkable tool… to help us best transmit our DNA. We are on Earth to perpetuate our genetic material, and for this we must live long enough to pass on the DNA of our cells to our descendants, and thus to defend ourselves, nourish ourselves, socialize, and find the right partners. This is the conviction I derive from reading evolutionary authors like Stephen Jay Gould or Richard Dawkins. It may seem like a disappointing answer to the riddle of the meaning of life. But what a liberating thought!

How does the cortex help us with this? By helping us react in the best possible way to what is about to happen in the near future.

Of course, it doesn't know the future, and nature doesn't know it either. What we do know, however, is that we live in a continuous world. That is, what will happen in the near future will closely resemble what happened in the near past. There are occasional changes, ruptures—for instance, one can change continents. One *can*, but, overall, what will happen in the near future is a reflection, or, in other words, coherent with what happened in the near past. Therefore, if we are able to have prepared ourselves and learned from the near past, we can use it to make predictions. If, in the future, I experience something analogous to a previous experience, by continuity of the world, I will expect something similar to happen next.

The cortex, via its maps, columns, and micro-columns, is precisely designed to analyze what happens to us, the experiences we live, and understand these experiences, by verifying whether we've already lived through similar ones. And if so, to remember what will happen next, the expected next step, and thus be capable of anticipating what will come. The brain is a prediction machine.

However, in the near past, the organism has lived through a large number of experiences—visual, sensory, all kinds of experiences, more or less repeated, frequent, significant, and more or less similar. It is not about finding an experience exactly as it was, since no two situations will never be exactly the same, but about understanding its framework, based on the essence of what is happening. The cortex must have memorized the essence of different situations.

Careful! By *essence*, I don't mean a vague word, a very abstract concept of the psychology of a situation, but very concrete axes of analysis that allow comparisons between lived experiences and gradually overvalue or undervalue the criteria based on their ability to distinguish a situation from those that resemble it. And, therefore, to gradually focus on what makes it possible to characterize a situation, which is its essence. This is the concept of analogy described by Sander and Hofstadter. I will return to this later.

These mechanisms of emergence of the essence of experiences do not resolve the question of their similarity: okay, the cortex has perceived what distinguishes the experience it is currently undergoing from another situation it has stored in memory, but should it consider them sufficiently similar to use them for making predictions, or not? Two other axes of analysis are used for this in addition to the similarity I just mentioned: a frequency axis and one I will call an impact axis.

The frequency axis takes into account how often this situation has been lived: once a month, once a year, once a decade? If you experience similar situations/experiences very often, it is important to be able to analyze them more carefully, to be able to segment them into several categories that resemble each other but are still distinct. This is the concept of expertise. A painter will know how to discriminate many more shades of color than an amateur. A sommelier or a perfumer will detect subtler smells and tastes than you or I—well, definitely myself—in a dominant odor that we categorize more roughly. A psychologist will know how to identify important weak signals in a situation that we might completely miss. Etc. Being exposed more frequently to a type of situation causes our cortical maps to segment these situations more finely, in order to label them with greater precision.

Now, the frequency axis alone is not enough: we also need to map the experiences based on the impact they had. If an experience is not very frequent but has a dire consequences, or on the contrary an extremely positive impact, our event analysis automate—the cortex and its cortical maps—must distinguish it from others and overvalue it. The cortex should not label this situation in the same way as many others that closely resemble it, but did not have the same impact, because the prediction resulting from it must be specific. To achieve this, the correlation with the emotions generated at that moment will be a useful key.

8. Wandering cortical maps

With these mechanisms for analyzing situations, by analogy with reference situations, which pave the space of all possible situations according to a granularity based on their frequency and impact, the brain can make relevant predictions and help the organism behave in the best way for itself. And it is the micro-columns, their interactions with other micro-columns in the same macro-column, neighboring macro-columns, and those of other cortical maps, that carry these mechanisms.

How do we combine the notion of expertise, which involves multiplying labels to characterize the most frequent lived situations, with the idea of a limited cortical surface, thus a limited number of micro-columns and columns? Do we have unused micro-columns and columns in the cortex, anticipating potential future specializations? The famous "only 10% of the brain" that is used?

Of course not!

The brain is the organ in the human body that consumes the most energy. It represents only 2% of our total body weight, yet consumes 25% of the organism's energy. It is the most energy-hungry part of our being. This shows how strong the selection pressure on it is. Every part of our brain must provide great utility to justify such a high energy consumption. Therefore, there is no question of parts of the cortex being underused. If it hasn't already been dispelled long ago, we must break with the idea that only 10% of our brain's potential is used under normal circumstances. On the contrary, our entire brain serves us continuously. But the art of using our brain is to constantly optimize the use of this finite surface that is the cortex based on its needs.

This implies that increasing expertise in a domain, thanks to the multiplication of lived experiences which translates into the increase in the number of labels in that domain, will also lead to a decrease in the number of labels elsewhere, thus decreasing expertise in other areas if we *make the hypothesis*, as I do, of a link between labels and cortical columns.

To visualize this phenomenon, let's first imagine a cortical map with a fixed number of labels. Let's say

400, for illustration. If 100,000 experiences lived by the organism activate cortical maps that themselves activate the one we're talking about, then each label on this map would represent 250 experiences, in the sense that each of the 250 experiences represented by a label would resemble that label more than any other. This is the very definition of labels. The label will be the best possible representative of these 250 experiences.

Now, let's imagine that the organism lives 100,000 new experiences, all very similar to each other and with the label L. Would this label L then become representative of 100,250 experiences, while each of the other 399 would still only represent 250? That would be a very poor use of the precious cortical surface which, in most experiences, would only be able to make a coarse prediction. On the other hand, a distribution of 500 experiences per label would give an optimal use of this cortical surface, with 200 of the labels dedicated to finely analyzing the 100,000 new experiences, and another 200 labels for the first 100,000 experiences. The map would increase its expertise in the region of experience space targeted by the new 100,000 experiences and decrease it elsewhere. Of course, the mechanism should be gradual, with each new experience slightly altering the coverage of the label space by the 400 labels on the map.

This is precisely a learning function: the labels of the cortical map, with a fixed number at this stage, evolve continuously to ensure that their collective set always best covers all the experiences lived by the organism.

And this happens in each cortical map in parallel.

This also adds a constraint to the cortical maps: if there is no direct link between maps, we could end up with very heavily used maps, such as those for musical notes, instruments, composers, and solfège for a musician, and, for example, other maps used very little if the person is not a hunter, blacksmith, or craftsman. Again, this would be a very poor use of the precious cortical surface.

A simple mechanism could compensate for this drift: for two adjacent maps, if the density of column use in one is higher than in the other, we would simply gradually transfer columns (or do so at the level of micro-columns) and thus the possibilities of labeling, from the least busy to the busiest, to balance things out.

I postulate this mechanism without being certain. I haven't read it anywhere; I don't know if others mention it. But it is entirely consistent with this model of the cortex, and has a visible consequence: by transferring cortical columns from one map to its neighbor, it's the cortical surface that is transferred. This means that, on an atlas representing the entire cortex, one map would be larger, and the neighboring one smaller—or not, if the one next to it was less used. In fact, the distribution of maps on the cortex would evolve over time, which I summarize as the shifting of maps, and the cortical atlas of different individuals would be different. The maps would not be in the same place or have the same size.

And it turns out that this is exactly what happens, what has been observed.[10] By the way, we can all do a thought experiment: what happens to the visual maps of a blind individual, which no longer receive input from the optic nerve? Do they become neutral unused areas? Of course not. Again, that would be a very poor use of the precious cortical surface. They are recycled, or rather gradually colonized by highly solicited maps that become more precise, more refined, more expert: touch, mathematics, etc.

This passage refers to the concept of experience in the sense of everything we, as human beings, have lived through. Incredibly adaptable, the cortex—despite being a uniform surface, structured the same way in every individual—evolves in a unique way in each person, and becomes so individualized that, beyond the primary maps, the cartography of the cortical maps is unique to each of us. No two individuals have the same cortical map atlas.

The differentiation of our cognitive abilities can also affect the primary level. It has been established experimentally that cats raised in cylinders with only vertical lines as stimuli will only recognize, on the primary layer of their perceptual apparatus, lines oriented in this way. Present them with diagonal or horizontal lines, and they won't see them. In our case, we humans recognize lines that are horizontal, vertical, and oriented at 16° intervals from one another. In the same way, we are used to seeing all colors, but we would be surprised to discover

---

10. Hubert R. Dinse, "Cortical Reorganization in the Aging Brain," *Progress in Brain Research* 157 (2006): 57-387.

the number of labels used for black, ochre, and red colors in Mali. Or, as Benjamin Lee Whorf said, for Eskimos, there are 23 different labels for white, but none for green.

Be careful, this does not imply that the green receptor no longer exists, as if in a type of color blindness. The variety of cones in the retina is not reduced; it is the micro-columns of area V1 that will have progressively weaker responses until they no longer react, like the cat that can't perceive an orientation other than vertical stripes. But in both cases, after a long period of readaptation, perception falls back in place.

This differentiation in our primary perceptual abilities is crucial in the context of sensitive periods early in life, when the expression of molecules critical to synaptic plasticity is strongest in sensory areas. Thus, it's easy for us to learn the distinctions in our culture, such as the sounds and phonemes of our native language early on in life, but acquiring them later is much more difficult.

9. SEMANTIC ENRICHMENT AND THE INCREASE IN INTEGRATION TIME

Now, what is the relationship between multiple cortical maps? Three phenomena occur when a cortical map transforms the flows it receives into labeled flows, meaning it places "tags" on more elementary co-occurring phenomena, phenomena that were happening simultaneously.

First, there's the fusion of flows. Illustrations of V1 or A1 cortical maps receiving receptive fields from the retina or cochlea, through which all characteristic phenomena are processed, might have led you to believe that a cortical map deals with simple, unique receptive fields.

I apologize if I made you think this, but it was just for the sake of demonstration. Because part of the power of the cortex actually comes from the opposite: a cortical map can—and generally does—receive multiple flows at once from several "lower-level" cortical maps, which are processed simultaneously, as well as from higher levels, since the "redescending" flows are far more numerous (even more so than ascending flows; we'll revisit this later). It's through the co-occurrence of features from multiple flows that a map can label much richer phenomena. It is by receiving a label from a lower-level map, such as "saw an elephant," from another map, "smell number XX," and from a third one, "gray shape moving to the right," and so on, that a higher-level map can characterize a global situation, a global configuration. Once transformed into labeled flows, following the cortex's "format," all flows can easily be considered based on their simultaneity. A cortical map that typically receives multiple flows at once is thus fusing sensors, modalities, and concepts, and gives rise to richer, more global concepts, which I sometimes refer to as a higher level of abstraction.

Next, and just as important, is integration time. The human brain has hardly evolved in the last several thousand years. It has gradually developed, structured itself, and adapted itself over tens of millions of years, long before the historical period. It wasn't designed to extract understanding from books, written words, screens, or charts that often present still images, but to process only evolving phenomena over time. Analyzing a phenomenon that evolves depends on the "observation time," or more precisely, the integration time. Take three photographs of a scene with a moving animal. One photo at one-hundredth of a second, one with a two-second pause, and another with a three-minute pause.

You won't see the same phenomena. Whether it's a zebra, an ant, or a cheetah, the first picture will be in focus, but you won't necessarily understand the animal's intent. In the second, the ant will have left a trace of its movement, and depending on their behavior (sleeping or hunting), the others may be blurry, sharp, or also trace their movement. Which you can analyze. In the third, the animals might no longer be present, but others will have appeared, offering you clues about the overall situation (a baby cheetah? A herd of zebras?).

The increase in integration time broadens access to other information, taking into account slower or successive phenomena. Each cortical map has its typical integration time, and the higher up you go in abstraction, meaning the more maps between the initial ones that receive raw sensory input from the "sensors of our senses," and the one we're discussing, the more the integration time increases. And this allows access to more global analyses of situations, both in their spatial and temporal composition. The cortical map analyzing a situation on a safari in Kenya may have received one label characterizing a herd of zebras grazing, another characterizing a pair of lionesses circling the herd from a distance, and yet another label identifying a pair of lions circling the herd of zebras and lurking in the distance downwind, and finally the label of a group of lions approaching the herd of zebras against the wind, a label received once the lionesses were in position. This analysis of the situation is quite high in the cortical map hierarchy, requiring a long integration time to perceive and characterize the different animals and their movements, and thus their tactical patterns.

It's no coincidence that science fiction authors like Liu Cixin, and many others, imagine multi-century or even multi-millennial timelines when creating their sagas. Ultimately, we all have the feeling that the world we are facing is accumulating layers of complexity unknown in the past. Not only are we dealing with the tactical patterns of daily life, and of history at a human scale, but other patterns—like climate evolution, the potential colonization of space, or scientific revolutions—give us a vague sense that the challenges we are facing have escalated.

Finally, the enrichment of labels, or rising abstraction. By definition, a cortical map labels, meaning it "names," a conjunction of co-occurring, more elementary phenomena that happen within a given period of time. It names this by searching its memory for the most analogous situation of the same type: "peaceful herd of zebras," "small group of lionesses moving discreetly downwind," "second group of lions moving into the opposite direction of the wind…" You've likely already understood where this is going: the first group of lions will make noise and rush toward the zebras, which will then rush toward the lionesses in ambush. It's a hunt. In fact, if you've understood this, it's because your cortex recognized it and already labeled it as a "zebra hunt." Your cortical maps don't need all the elements of the scene to label it. They spend their time trying to label what's happening with just a few elements, through analogy.

By the way, if I used labels like "small group of lionesses moving discreetly downwind" to illustrate rising abstraction, with a richness of description, this does not correspond at all the type of labels the cortex uses. The new label is not in any way a *grammatically* combined set of labels from the phenomena that led to its emergence; it is instead coded neurally, primarily through the size of the synapses, or the augmentation in diameter of the axons, or of new connections—new synapses between neurons. The size of the synapses, highly sensitive to co-occurrence, explains the increase in synaptic efficiency, as the number of receptors automatically increases with synapse volume. This is the basis of synaptic plasticity; other evolutions occur only in the first years of life.

10. THE FEEDBACK MORE IMPORTANT THAN THE ASCENDING PATH

All the examples and illustrations I've used so far have concerned perception. Would the cortical functioning model I've presented here only work with perception? No, not at all. That was just to push the topic until it became easier to address. In fact, there is no distinction between action maps and perception maps, between those connected to the spinal cord and those connected to the eyes. Furthermore, the separation between perception and action is quite artificial, as muscles continuously send information about their state and position directly to the cortical map that controls them, and perception maps, such as the V1 visual map, also send commands to the eye muscles, as vision is intrinsically linked to eye saccades. Even better, the entire interaction between cortical maps I've presented works in both directions.

The "ascending" or feedforward path, as it is called, involves neurons that receive inputs indirectly from the retina, for example, and propagate their activations to other higher-level neurons, then to others still. This path is not the only one in the cortex. In fact, it is a minority: there are nine times more feedback neurons, thus descendant circuits, than ascending circuits.

I propose we understand these proportions in at least three ways: as a counter-reaction to improve perception, as a filter for intentionality, and as a virtual reconstruction.

The counter-reaction involves "sending back" to the input what has been understood, for instance, to the V1 visual area, to compare it to what is perceived and use the differences to enhance understanding. I illustrate this with a dialogue between two cortical maps:

> "Hello, this is number 1. In the noisy signal I'm receiving, I detected three right angles and two equal lines, plus some line segments. Does this ring a bell?
> — This is n+1 (with a bit of pride). That could correspond to a square, but we'd also need a right angle over here, and more consistent lines here.

> — This is number 1. Yes, I vaguely detect something at the angle; that could be one. And the line segments I had detected are roughly along the path of the line you're looking for. We can validate.
> — This is n+1. *Roger, roger,* that, it's definitely a square!"

The counter-reaction, which significantly strengthens perception, reduces the need to enhance the precision of sensory sensors. It's an excellent saving for the organism, but it requires descending pathways.

However, a trap lies in this mechanism, which leads to a major simplification: the size of what is perceived must match the size of what was memorized for comparison. If it's hard to compare an object seen from far away with one memorized up close, the cortex simplifies the situation by introducing a scale invariance; all the elements in a scene are analyzed and memorized at the same scale. A simple test will make you aware of this: close your eyes and visualize the following list of items: a lemon, a house, an elephant, a banana.

I bet you visualized them all at the same size... All the elements are mentally perceived at the same scale, the elephant like the banana, because they are "stored" at the same scale. It's feedback that introduces this scale invariance. And the primary energy-saving due to feedback is in processing elements at the correct scale, while everything else is ignored.

The intentionality filter relates to a completely different subject. How is the cortex's machinery used? In two ways: open, in standby mode, with no intention, just perceiving what's happening around you; or in a directed way, with an intention (I'm looking for keys, trying to hear where my daughter is hiding...). In this case of intentionality, the higher cortical maps that code what we're searching for (keys) send the component elements (rings, metal discs with rectangular shapes, textured areas) to the lower maps; they transmit the specific criteria (sequences of angles and small line segments in alternating directions). Each perception map analyzes the signals it receives but limits its perceptual field to the sought elements. This is why, as soon as part of these elements appears in our field of vision, they immediately grab our attention. Meanwhile, while focused on finding the keys, we don't notice anything else. Descending pathways are necessary for this, too. And incidentally, if someone asks you, "While you were looking for your keys, didn't you happen to find my glasses?"—then not a chance!

A counting experiment bridges the intentionality filter and virtual reconstructions. The experiment involves placing observers in front of a TV screen showing a basketball game between a one team clad in white and another dressed in black. The number of players on both teams is non-standard, unknown, and the observer is asked to watch the game for a few minutes and count how many players are dressed in white. Of course, the players are moving around in all directions, passing in front of each other, and counting the whites requires focus. At the end, the observer is asked how many they counted and then asked if they saw the gorilla. "What gorilla???"

Upon re-watching the game, they realize that, in the middle of the screen, a person dressed as a gorilla, all in black, walked through. It was impossible to miss, yet the observer did. About 50% of observers miss the gorilla. Their attention was focused on the white players.

This is known as an attention test. You can find videos of these experiments online, even if being warned, you'd probably spot the gorilla now. But there might still be a surprise for you... There are many such attention tests, and they show just how much our analysis of scenes or situations involves reconstructions that are far from a simple passive recording of available data[11].

In fact, it's as though your cortex doesn't analyze information coming directly from the outside world, but instead from a virtual world that it recreates by using some sensory information to complete and anchor it in reality, but filtered according to the information it needs.

What I'm telling you here is that what you're seeing right now is not the real world, but a virtual world that your brain is constantly recreating, and your vision only serves to connect it to the real world. It's a real eye-opener, right? But that's what's happening. In addition, when you dream, your brain creates very real worlds. The same happens when you close your eyes and visualize internal images. And this requires a lot of descending neurons.

11. For example "Testez votre attention sélective en deux minutes chrono" (Test your selective attention in two minutes flat), Frédéric Castaignède, *Demain l'école, Episode 2: Du bon usage du cerveau* (Arte and Effervescence Doc), 2018. <https://www.youtube.com/watch?v=E-pLmE3u-HGc&ab_channel=Telerama>. Daniel Simons, YouTube: <https://www.youtube.com/watch?v=IGQmdoK_ZfY>.

This is the concept of the brain as a world creator, developed by (again) Alain Berthoz. It explains why there are nine times more bits of descending information "from your brain" to your visual maps than information ascending from your eyes to your brain. You don't see with your eyes; you see with your brain. The same applies to all your faculties of perception and action.

11. The hierarchy of cortical maps, brain loops

To complete this overview of how the cortex works, we must mention the structure of the network of cortical maps, which are connected by bidirectional links, and increase in richness, abstraction, and integration time as we move away from the primary sensory input/output maps. But this says nothing about their organization, nor which map is connected to which other, or why. Yves Burnod, research director at CNRS-INSERM, and his wife Niki, have written a book[12] on this topic. I refer you to it if you wish to explore the question further. First, because I lack the knowledge and expertise to discuss these issues, and second, because this would greatly exceed the scope of this book. Their book deals with cortical map cascades organized into seven major brain networks, seven loops that unfold in the brain and specialize in seven main areas of competence, such as vital, social, and verbal skills. What they call the "atlas of skills" facilitates the acquisition of core competencies, such as those required for gestures or

12. Y. Burnod and N. Burnod, *The Panoramic Brain*, *op. cit.*

language. The topic is fascinating and too vast to be included in this book, but I found it important to position the theme here.

12. Conclusion: equality of intelligences before nature

In fact, the cortex might *a priori* be simpler than we initially think, and like modern-day Mountcastles, by approaching it with an obsession to find simple mechanisms, we might discover the unifying framework we've been missing.

When I read that "the human brain is the most complex object in the known universe" (Christof Koch, 2012, an American neuroscientist who has been quoted by many media), in addition to the incredible arrogance of the statement, I understand that those people, based on the principle of complexity, will never figure out how the brain works. They will look for complex solutions.

In short, sometimes I feel that the brain is opaque because we don't want to understand it, that we want to preserve the mysterious, obscure part of what makes us human. By the way, when we ask, ChatGPT, which in a sense synthesizes all that's said on various networks, how the brain works, it invariably responds that it is incredibly complex. Because the brain is in part linked to thought, we would feel humiliated to look at it in a simple, mechanistic way, as Darwin, Sun Tzu, or Machiavelli might. Descartes posited a union of the soul and body and located in the pineal gland. I believe the mechanistic view is the correct one.

I think all brains are alike. They all work the same way, although each of us has a uniquely different perception of the world. Faced with the same music, a jazz musician hears countless nuances, intervals, and harmonic patterns, while the rest of us struggle to identify the basic melody. A Guardiola, a Mourinho, and an Ancelotti watch a soccer match like it's a chess game, studying the rebounds with the same attention to detail that fans of Harry Potter apply to the latest installment of their favorite series. As for me, I have the ability to visualize a robot's inner structure where someone who spends a considerable amount of time in cafés will probably only see an automaton that's a bit clumsy. But that likely has a sharp memory for names and the ability to detect subtle social cues that would completely elude me in the unfamiliar jungle of their regular haunt.

It's the sum of all our experiences—what we've lived, read, heard, felt—that has shaped the filter through which we analyze the present, our cortex. And I believe that, at least among mammals, we can say exactly the same thing, except that because their cortex is smaller, their ability to "abstract" and integrate over longer periods of time is weaker. But the functioning of their cortex is likely identical.

Among humans, I firmly believe in the equality of intelligence before nature. We all develop our intellectual talents according to our needs, tastes, and the time we allocate to challenges that stimulate us. But we can't cover all domains. Brain plasticity plays out within the surface of the cortex, which seems fixed once and for all, with its stable number of micro-columns and neurons. In this sense, the brain is a remarkable machine of simplicity. Amid all the noise that makes up our experience, it becomes accustomed to spotting and processing the configurations and evolution of signal structures that are useful and familiar to us. It ultimately shapes a world in our image, filtering it according to our intentions, indirectly through the prism of our lived experiences. All of this it does to ensure our survival and reproduction in a jungle of tactical and strategic processes that constantly threaten us. Some parts of the cortex are dedicated to social interactions, others to rational subjects, and still others to philosophical and conceptual matters. The proportions of these areas differ between individuals. This may be what some refer to as emotional intelligence, conceptual intelligence, and other related forms.

Finally, if I were to provide an overall indicator of intelligence, I would suggest the surface area of the cortex relative to size, which is probably the same for everyone… Or maybe not.

3

Surviving through tactical patterns

One Sunday afternoon, you're driving your car calmly, returning from a friend's house, when suddenly, on the right, a kid runs out into the street. Disaster. You slam on the brakes, gripping the steering wheel tightly, the tires screech... Whew, you manage to stop just in time, with nothing more than a shared scare. What a relief. But wait a moment: how long did it take for you to react? To detect the sudden appearance of the child, figure out what was happening, and, most importantly, anticipate what would happen next, decide to slam on the brakes, release the accelerator to push down the brake pedal, and grip the steering wheel to avoid being thrown into the windshield. About one-tenth of a second. That's pretty quick for a reaction time. Well done. And when you think that it's neurons, the basic components of the brain, organized in micro-columns, that are responsible for this... Quite an impressive system. But... hold on a second... neurons are slow! It takes them between five and seven milliseconds to react to a stimulus and "trigger," to respond. Which means that during the tenth of a second it took for you to detect and avoid the disaster, at most about twenty neurons were involved, one after the other? What calculation power they must have! Not exactly, because many neurons were likely working in parallel, several "chains of twenty neurons" functioning simultaneously, intertwining and feeding each other. Nonetheless, chains of up to twenty neurons maximum. And in twenty steps of a low-level programming language, there's no time to do anything, and no matter how many times you put large quantities of "no time to do anything" *in parallel*, in the end, it won't do anything!

But if the brain didn't have time to calculate, it still had time to search its memory, searched for a lot of things simultaneously. Have I ever seen something appear like that and move at that speed? Yes; and what was the subsequent trajectory, what were the next steps? And me, as I move and perceive my own motion, what will my next step be? Oh no, collision… Among all the sequences of movements recorded in my cortex, which ones led to the next step of stopping the car? Okay, I'll trigger that sequence. Triggering this sequence leads to searching for the next steps in this new sequence unfolding, because it doesn't matter whether it's me or the external world that caused it. The next steps are stopping the car, okay, but also me being thrown into the windshield, etc.

A simple mechanism based on identifying (or "labeling") the current sequence, searching memory for an analogous sequence, and retrieving the next step from the remembered analogous sequence allows us, without any calculations, to "predict"—as long as this sequence, or something analogous to it, has already been memorized. A second, equally simple mechanism allows us to identify a sequence from a situation (a label), find a sequence where this label is one of the next steps, and use that to trigger an appropriate reaction, without any calculations either.

In conclusion, under certain conditions, which I would express as "you've learned how to drive and already had some driving experience," meaning you've memorized sequences, and "the system knows how to recognize the essence of a situation" because we're never exactly in the same situation, and "the system knows how to retrieve something from memory by accessing its content," under these conditions, you can save the kid without much calculation, just with a "twenty-step system."

The foundation of this chapter, and the Organic AI model, are deeply structured by what this example tells us: our brain doesn't have time to calculate responses to the situations that arise, yet it still provides them. The model of a tactical pattern offers a response and draws consequences from it.

1. What is a tactical pattern?

The idea of "tactical pattern" came to me when I read Jeff Hawkins's book *On Intelligence*, which really clicked for me. You know, those moments when you think, "damn, but of course!" and find a response, or a formulation, for something that has been on your mind for a long time but that you just couldn't quite pinpoint. It revolves around a powerful idea that we rarely touch upon in AI: the concept of "sequence of situations," "sequence of configurations," or "sequence of patterns," which I ultimately named "tactical patterns," even if I switch between these terms depending on the context.

I'm referring here to successions of perceived things, linked together, unfolding in our field of consciousness. A succession of sounds, noises, heard words, evolving smells, the sequence of imprints on our retina and cortex, from the sight of a bird flying or a dog running to the sensations of touch from a caress; or, at more abstract levels, it could be a succession of steps in a tactical pattern in rugby, soccer, or hockey, or a mathematical proof... in short, a sequence of configurations unfolding.

The term "tactical pattern" differs from that of "pattern sequence" used by Jeff Hawkins, because the latter only suggests a succession of motifs or figures, without purpose, without an "end goal." That's the essence of these sequences. However, it often happens that the sequence of configurations is punctuated by key stages; it leads somewhere, to a result, a goal, a final situation that can be recognized just like the starting situation. And it can be the object of intention. "Tactical pattern" seems more appropriate in these cases, although it may feel a bit overblown when applied to situations like the sequence of gestures for drying off after a shower, or the flight of a bird. We'll see this soon, and I'll use these terms alternately depending on the case.

2. "Everything is a tactical pattern"

In a way, everything is a tactical pattern.

Let's go back to the example of lions in the savanna. A herd of antelopes is grazing, and the wind is blowing. A group of lionesses makes a wide detour to position themselves downwind, along the route the herd will take in its flight, while other lions quietly move closer and position themselves upwind, ahead of the antelopes in the direction of the breeze. To a keen observer, these stealthy movements, maneuvers to encircle, divisions, and regroupings of the pride are parts of a larger structure, carrying essential information: a hunt is about to take place.

Thus, around us, tactical patterns unfold constantly. While I'm writing this page, a bird flies past the window. Its silhouette oscillates at regular frequencies, its wings beat cyclically, but I don't notice. It's a "non-event" that my brain has seen, as it entered my field of perception, then analyzed and labeled by one of the many "twenty-step pathways" that unfold massively in parallel within my cortex; but it's deemed unimportant since all the predictions made by this twenty-step pathway were verified, thus without surprise—"nothing new here"—nor does it correspond to something being sought (if I were in "intentional" mode, meaning looking for something, my brain would have been alerted as soon as a prediction matched the intention), so I don't pay attention to it. But if by magic the bird had suddenly disappeared, my attention would have been drawn to it, because something would have happened. My brain would have immediately interrupted my writing: it would have noticed a movement, broken it down into a sequence of patterns, found similar pattern sequences in my memory, and then gone on to search for the next step of this analogous sequence and compared it to the new situation, since the movement had advanced a bit while this search was taking place; as long as the comparison was positive, it was a normal, standard movement, not requiring attention. But when the bird vanished, that was no longer normal; something demanded attention. And our attention was drawn to the phenomenon. "Something happened."

Much earlier, when I got out of the shower, I was thinking about something else and was using my towel to dry off. I realized I was still doing it the same way, in the same order, drying off with a fairly invariant routine, a sequence of gestures performed almost automatically.

It's the same mechanism that allows us to race down stairs at full speed without having to calculate where each foot lands at every moment. If we tried to think about the placement of our feet while speeding down the steps, it would surely be a disaster. Calculating, thinking about where to place our feet takes too much time for us to continue at the same speed.

Fragments of sequences are embedded in our brain and let us move through parts of the present moment almost automatically, as if carried along a conveyor belt. These fragments are stored somewhere, ready to be unrolled when needed. That somewhere is the cortex. It's thanks to these tactical patterns that we were able to brake and avoid the kid at the start of this chapter without the cortex doing any calculations. In any case, it wouldn't have had time. That's the challenge of intelligence.

Some tactical patterns are obvious, so much so that we no longer see them, that they have become almost unconscious. Others are invisible, accessible only to experienced brains. I vibrate, I see a collection of dots moving, I cheer for my favorite soccer team when they score a goal. But if I watch the replay, the cameras recorded a collective arrangement, its progression on the billiard-like surface of the field. Arrows, halos, and slow-motion shots help break down this movement into different phases, giving it a familiar, repeatable quality that allows spectators to briefly share the coach's perspective; to decode the tactical pattern that the players had learned and executed on screen. Experience gradually teaches them to recognize when a movement begins, when there's danger, or when they can run to grab a can of something to drink from the fridge, with a minimal risk of missing something. It's the same for lions hunting antelopes.

In the end, "Reality" can be seen as a vast tactical pattern; or more precisely, *we can ask whether intelligence is merely a manager of tactical patterns*, whether the cortex sees the world only through the lens of tactical patterns. These sequences of situations appear even in the most unsuspected places, although they're not always easy to recognize at first glance: recognizing, for example, the configurations, repetitions, and evolutions, and therefore the tactical patterns, in a piece of jazz or a game of chess, requires high specialization and a long learning process, and demands a highly specialized brain.

Understanding and feeling the strategy of a strangler fig involves an analysis over ten years or more. Fortunately, we can occasionally see snapshots of the fig at different stages of its tactical pattern and reconstruct the overall scheme. It's a tactical pattern seen in hindsight, but that's okay. And reconstructing the whole scheme from fragments perceived here and there requires already having perceived similar tactical patterns, albeit on a different scale.

On the one hand, we struggle to integrate long durations, because our perceptual and conceptual apparatus is geared toward short-term experiences, with time constants that aren't well-suited. On the other hand, it takes time to recognize the subtleties of processes outside the margins of our usual experience: the behavior of certain animals, and even more so of plants, the evolutions of history or climate, all belong to this side.

3. What are the advantages and limitations of such "tactical" intelligence?

The issue of pattern flows and pattern sequences is interesting because, in this framework, the brain doesn't need to be a calculator—just a memory that records and retrieves sequences of patterns. For example, when listening to music, we immediately recognize a melody even if it's played in a different key or at a slower pace. I can hum *Frère Jacques* starting on any note, at any "speed," and you will instantly recognize the tune. However, if I don't sing in the "official" key, all the notes will be different! If I don't sing in the right tempo, the entire sequence will be altered! This means we don't recognize pitch or notes separately, but rather the sequence of variations. That's what we recognize: the sequence of variations. Variation in pitch, tempo, inter-note timing…

The same almost applies to vision. When we look at a face, our eyes don't stay fixed analyzing its entirety; they make rapid eye saccades three times per second without us noticing, quickly moving from one eye to the other, to the nose, mouth, back to the eyes, and to specific features of the face… They scan the points of attention in the visual field, focusing on those that stand out due to contrast, shape, color, or displacement; it doesn't matter how this point is distinguished from the rest of the visual field, but the gaze constantly moves from one to the other. These eye movements are the fastest of any muscles in the human body, and the ocular muscles are the ones with the most position sensors, allowing them to give very precise information about the movement they just made and the relative difference in position.

Furthermore, precise vision is very focused: the zone of the retina with the highest "pixel" density is called the fovea, and it corresponds to the field of vision of a two-euro coin held at arm's length! It's only in this area that we see precisely, and it's actually quite small! The pixels here are essentially materialized in cones, the retinal cells that detect color, with a small proportion of rods. Surrounding it, as you move away from the fovea's center, the proportion of cones rapidly decreases in favor of rods, which are more sensitive to low light intensities but only see in black and white. Also, pixel density decreases quickly, so the image becomes blurrier. For example, our vision is only one-tenth of its sharpness at 20°: if you look at the edge of your TV from a normal distance (2.5 to 3 meters), you can vaguely make out the opposite edge with an acuity of less than a tenth! We only see clearly in the center of our eye; it's a very focused vision, and what our eyes see is actually a series of highly focused, localized visions that the brain uses to reconstruct the world it perceives. This is similar to the sequence of variations perceived in sound, where pitch, tempo, and inter-note variations are replaced by the characterizations of each significant point: the differences between parts, relative dimensions… That's what we recognize—not a global view of a face as it would appear in a photo. We recognize sequences of configurations without order!

For each face perceived, a new unordered sequence of patterns has been detected. This raises a large issue about labeling, categorization, and analogy…

In fact, memorizing a face to remember it later means memorizing this sequence of patterns. However, even though you may see the same face many times, it will never correspond exactly to the same sequence: hair that is longer, shorter, styled differently, windblown; three-day stubble; a tan; seen from different angles, under different lighting, with different facial expressions, etc. Since it's impossible to memorize all sequences for each face, it's necessary to identify all sequences corresponding to the same face as being the same; hence, the concept of resemblance between sequences and categories: this set of tactical patterns groups sequences that are sufficiently similar so that they belong to the same category, that of Mr. or Mrs. X's face. It's enough to memorize a typical pattern sequence for this category—the essence of what characterizes these sequences, which I call the archetypal sequence—so that any new face pattern sequence can be compared to it and determine if the faces match: it is indeed Mrs. X.

Or more precisely, determine if the difference between the pattern sequence we perceive and Mrs. X's archetypal sequence is small enough to consider the person as Mrs. X. It's the same thing, but not quite exactly the same: this opens up the possibility that other people, thus different from Mrs. X, but with a small enough deviation from her archetypal sequence, could also be recognized as Mrs. X. There's a misidentification! Do we have a specific category for each person we've met? Is there a minimum difference between several pattern sequences below which we can't tell them apart?

These questions brought several enlightening memories to mind, starting with the memory of a person I saw on the street and remarked aloud to the person I was walking with that he looked a bit like Brad Pitt, that he had the same type of face. "Not at all!" responded my neighbor. "He looks more like Matt Damon…" And I wondered: how can we see the same person and each find a strong resemblance but with different people, whom we were both familiar with and who don't really look alike? Then I recalled other experiences in Lyon, the city where I grew up in the 1970s and 1980s. At that time, the mix of human types in France's second-largest conurbation was fairly low: I rarely encountered Asians. I thought they all looked alike. But years later, after traveling around Asia, through various regions of China, Japan, Korea, Malaysia, and Singapore, I quickly learned to distinguish between Japanese, Korean, and Chinese faces. It was as if, when I saw few Asians, I had only one category for all of them, which grouped all the pattern sequences of the faces I encountered. As my experiences expanded, this catch-all category split into several specialized ones. Each category had its representative, both as the flagbearer of the category but also as the face that best resembled all the individuals in that category—sort of a synthesis of the regrouped pattern sequences, the representative of the archetypal sequence of the category. Depending on the experiences lived by each person, in terms of all the faces we've seen in our life and the order in which we've seen them, our categories will be different, with different representatives. The same new face seen by you and me might not be categorized the same way, and we would recognize in it different resemblances to different archetypal faces.

I emphasize this example of faces because it's very illustrative of a phenomenon that applies to everything: what we perceive, whether passive or dynamic scenes, seems to be perceived as sequences of patterns. Identifying these patterns involves finding the category with the most *similar* archetypal sequence, and labeling what we've perceived as belonging to that category. These categories evolve with experience, becoming more refined and expert with the concentration of encounters they've been shaped by—this is what we call learning. However, this categorization is very different from neural Networks, and owes more to the analogies specified by Sander and Hofstadter than to clustering, that is, the segmentation of all possibilities into discrete categories. This topic will be discussed later on in this book.

4. But then, if everything follows a tactical pattern, referencing something already experienced, where does creativity fit in?

I have an attempt at an explanation through tactical patterns. One that requires going back to basics to be understood. Let's recall that the brain is a kind of sponge inside a black box, the skull. It knows nothing about the world outside the box and only receives signal flows through the nerves; some come from the eyes via ganglia, others from the ears and from other body sensors. Between the sensors themselves and the arrival in the cortex, the signals pass through intermediate modules, ganglia or others, where they are somewhat standardized. Thus, the cortex itself receives standardized signals from various channels, and it doesn't know whether they come from the eyes, ears, or elsewhere. It only receives signal flows that all have the same structure. These flows are analyzed and managed as sequences of patterns; one sequence could come from the last symphony you listened to, another from the sensation of bitter cold you felt when riding your snowmobile to a concert in a blizzard, the sting of snowflakes on your reddened face; yet another from the warmth and burning sensation caused by the shot of whiskey you took from your flask to fight the cold. Everything generates sequences of patterns that your cortex analyzes, compares to existing ones, records directly or as an evolution of the closest existing pattern sequence. But they are all stored in the same format. And the question you face at a given moment might find its solution as the next step in a pattern sequence derived from a completely different experience… It's the tactical pattern perceived during a symphony, a soccer match, or a game of chess that helps you find the next movement in the detective novel you're writing, or the inspiration for the global dynamics of the painting you're working on. Or it's the chain of tactical patterns that helps you make progress in a mathematical proof. This amounts to transposing a progression dynamic from one field to a completely different one.

Thus, ultimately, we would be more creative the more we've *lived*, or more precisely, *been exposed to,* different situations—different types and modalities—throughout our lives?

Maybe it's not so strange after all…

But there's a second layer to the rocket: the more experiences we live, the more the synapses encoding configuration sequences grow; and the larger the synapses become, the more they synthesize "spontaneous" proteins that activate them without any direct causality. This is a significant property of neurotransmitter release in the synapse; it's a creator's chance event, but controlled by what we learn. Creativity also resides at the molecular level, boosted by learning, i.e., exposure to more situations, more experiences.

Following the thread of creativity leads me to the shores of current generative models, one of whose weaknesses is integrating the laws of physics. For generated images or videos to be realistic—i.e., at least consistent with the physics we experience every moment—a stone thrown into deep space should go straight, but a stone thrown on Earth should curve towards the ground in the correct way. Following the laws of physics, which generative models don't know, given their operating principles. The pattern sequence model, viewed and learned as relationships of correlation between situations that follow each other in the real world and the consequences that also occur in the real world, inherently incorporates the laws of physics. The sequences of positions or developments of real phenomena have already been subjected to these laws of physics...

5. Tactical patterns supporting strategic foresight

Since my childhood, I have loved science fiction because it allows us to think, thanks to the works of the most brilliant authors, about the future of technology, but also because it challenges us with issues that are at the level of our history. The plot of *The Three-Body Problem* allows us to seriously ask what we would do if we were to discover the existence of extraterrestrial civilizations. But it also offers a vital reflection on how our societies respond to challenges that unfold over the long term—challenges similar to those we are facing today, such as the ecological crisis, climate change, and geopolitical instability, or in other words, phenomena of great complexity, inscribed in long-term timeframes, to which responses can only be multifactorial.

In this regard, I believe that the concept of a tactical pattern allows us to approach foresight reasoning on *rational grounds, considering history as a reservoir of models full of lessons for the future.* This might sound like a cliché—"history is full of lessons for the future..."—but when seen through the lens of situational sequences, it takes on a different meaning: doesn't the tactical pattern unfolding right now already have an analogue recorded somewhere in the cortex? Whether related to phenomena of the same type, or of a completely different type: for instance, it could be a scheme similar to a chess game I once played, or to the tactical pattern of a wolf pack hunting a herd of wild horses, as I discovered in Jiang Rong's excellent book *Wolf Totem*, which inspired a film by Jean-Jacques Annaud. In these cases, the cortex can predict what will happen and anticipate it simply by examining the sequence of the tactical pattern, without needing to perform any calculations. It is said that the brain does not *calculate*, it *represents*. That's the mechanism. Jiang Rong's book also suggests that the military tactics of Genghis Khan's Mongols—who fought armies much larger than their own—were inspired by the observation of wolves. Wolves were the great predators of their steppes, and attacked their herds of livestock; against hordes of horses that were far from inoffensive and much larger than they were. The Mongols had the opportunity to encounter wolves. This is the transposition of analogous tactical patterns...

We can follow this thought further: I have always been interested in history, or more precisely, the dynamics of history—not the dates and isolated events like the succession of kings' names or isolated incidents, but the great movements and currents of history. In this respect, I was very surprised during my first visit to China to discover the invasions of the Xiongnu, regular invasions and raids between

200 BCE and 200 CE by nomadic peoples from the steppes of Mongolia and Southern Siberia. It was precisely to defend against them that the Great Wall of China began to be built. I was surprised because it was from the same region that the Mongols who invaded China came, and much of Eurasia a thousand years later. And in our European civilizations, our regular invaders came from the northeast of Europe, from the vast Eurasian steppe, while invaders from Southeastern Europe and the Middle East came from their own northeast, also from the great steppe. This was already seen in ancient Egypt and Greece. There seems to be a common pattern emerging: regularly, nomadic peoples from the vast Eurasian steppe (Scythians, Xiongnu, Mongols, and others…) were in a state of excess population and excitement, sweeping over the peripheral sedentary civilizations in waves. Generally, these nomadic groups would win, and they would assimilate into these civilizations, which would eventually absorb them, picking up a few marginal developments along the way. This pattern is common to the Huns, Vikings, Alans, Alamanni, Xiongnu, Mongols, etc.

It is also extremely interesting to correlate these historical movements with climatic phenomena: one discovers warmer periods that saw an increase in the population of nomads from the steppes, and other colder periods that contributed to the growth of populations in desert areas (fourth century Arabian Peninsula, for example…). More tactical patterns to establish. But that is another story.

Ultimately, the entire set of these same tactical patterns, or similar schemas, applied to a range of situations—such as all the peoples of the Eurasian steppes, all the locations of the steppe, and all the different periods in time—offers us a systemic view of a phenomenon.

As if a systemic view emerges from the perception of a set of correlated tactical patterns.

The history of civilizations can be approached in the same way. Instead of a list of dates and events recounting the rise of civilization and writing in Mesopotamia, Egypt, China, and India, one might prefer the approach of systemic logic. What do we see then? Whether we look at the Sahara, the Gobi Desert, or the Near East: we know that more than 11,700 years ago, before the Holocene, the current interglacial period, the climate was colder everywhere on Earth. With the rise in temperatures at the start of the Holocene, and despite some climate oscillations, these areas became vast green spaces with lakes, abundant animals, and life—including humans. Then, as the climate continued to warm, leading to desertification around the world, the climate pushed living beings from these areas toward the periphery of the now-dry regions, near the areas that remained wet, such as the great lakes and rivers, creating demographic concentration zones. For example, along the great rivers. These concentrations were conducive to sedentarization, the division of roles, the organization of society, the emergence of priests, clergy, and thus religions, and the development of civilization. This can be observed almost everywhere at the same time, some five to six thousand years ago. A little earlier here, a little later there, but roughly speaking, at the same time on the time scale of civilizations, advanced civilizations and often writing emerged along the Yellow River in China, along the Nile in Egypt, between the Tiber and the Euphrates in Mesopotamia, but also in Turkey, Niger, or along the Indus. In all the cradles of civilization. The same pattern that, although applied to different situations and places, explains why civilizations appeared everywhere at almost the same time. A systemic view.

The more we are able to spot strategies over long periods, the more we can detect the processes at work in the present and anticipate the future. And of course, it is at the level of the cortical maps of the highest abstraction, in the frontal cortex, and even further ahead in the frontal cortex, that long integration times allow us to memorize and detect increasingly long tactical patterns.

In the early 2000s, a friend working at Danone in China had visited one of his suppliers in Mongolia. On the walls of the director's office, there was a large map of Eurasia crossed by three large arrows: the plans for the three successive waves of conquest launched from Asia toward Europe—those of Genghis Khan, Timur, and… the one to come. For these leaders, current development strategies might simply be a reworking of tactical patterns already implemented by Timur or Genghis Khan. Meanwhile, we, unaware of this history, see the economic expansion of these Asian giants as just another manifestation of market capitalism.

When we fail to recognize an adversary's tactical pattern, as is the case with the giant trees in the Amazon and the strangler fig, the process, in its slow way, inevitably leads to a fatal outcome. This is why AI systems capable of spotting tactical patterns beyond the analytical scope of our intelligence would collectively increase our chances of survival while making us more subtle. With climate change, migratory dynamics and the shift of the culture of olive groves or vineyards to northern Europe announce historical processes that will unfold over decades or centuries. How can we assess the impact of the choices we make today at such scales, and how can we make informed decisions without artificial intelligences capable of modeling their consequences and comparing different long-term scenarios?

6. The question touched upon episodically but not addressed of categories and analogies

An important reflection on the labeling of tactical patterns or pattern sequences is whether a newly perceived sequence is *found* (to use a generic term) in a category and can thus be labeled by that category. In fact, it's the question of what a category encompasses…

As I have already mentioned, three criteria need to be considered to determine what is grouped within a category: an idea of the frequency of the appearance of sequences, the similarity between members of the category, and their significance.

Frequency relates to the depth of analysis and deals with an axis ranging from catch-all to expertise. Repositioning the brain in its context of helping its owner survive in a world of continuity, where the near future will not be very different from the recent past, expertise on what happens often will allow the brain to distinguish subtle variants in frequent situations. It's almost about detecting weak signals that allow one to differentiate between two situations that look alike, but someone who is experienced in these situations will be able to tell the difference. Therefore, it is better to have several categories, even ones that are fairly close to each other, to describe frequent situations. This is the example I mentioned earlier of Asian faces, for example, all looking the same to me, which meant they were in the same category as I hadn't seen many of them, and then, as the number of encounters with Asian people increased, this category split into several.

The notion of significance aims to modulate frequency discrimination based on the emotional impact of a situation. For example, I'm scuba diving and catch a glimpse of a large shadow moving in the corner of my eye. Such an event would be unsettling for any diver, and my brain might instinctively classify it as the kind of encounter that belongs to a unique tactical pattern — the kind where I reflexively flee from an imagined threat. But in reality, it's a whale giving birth. And rather than fear, I experience a particularly powerful emotional reaction. (Maybe you expected a shark. I deliberately avoided that tired cliché, which I find irritating, since we now know that sharks are mostly peaceful animals, responsible for far fewer accidents each year than hippopotamuses, kangaroos, dogs, or even cows. Yet they continue to be cast as villains, terrifying predators we imagine must be driven from the oceans. Hollywood and Steven Spielberg deserve, to my mind, to be condemned for crimes against nature.) But in trying to make a good job of it, I watered down my example… Let's start over. The thief who suddenly appears in your hallway gives a particular emphasis to the sequence of events that happened just before, so much so that you overvalue what took place in order to be prepared for the next time this sequence, although extremely rare, occurs. This is equally true for strong negative and positive emotions, which cause us to overvalue the sequences that led to them, thereby creating categories that are sparsely populated.

Finally, the notion of similarity, a question that is at the same time simpler and more complex. It's quite simple for us to say that two situations resemble each other, or that two animals resemble each other, or that two trees resemble each other, but it's not simple to list the criteria that must be identical. Well not identical, but sufficiently close and similar. Think simply of a table. What criteria should be compared to say that what you see is a table? Four legs and a tabletop? But there are tables with all kinds of leg configurations: one, three, six… At least one leg then? I've picnicked on a tree stump, on a plank placed on two swings… or even on a plank placed on the ground. Okay, let's drop the legs and focus on the tabletop: but I know plenty of furniture that isn't a table yet has what could be considered a tabletop. A buffet? A stool? A podium? Or even an architect's table? Oops, so that won't work either; and I didn't even get into multiplication tables, which are indeed tables. So, let's focus on the use: a mostly flat object on which I place something to eat? Would a car hood we use for a picnic be a table then?

The open trunk of a car? … I started with a simple example, a table, and I'm struggling to determine the criteria that allow us to objectively label a new object as a table. Sometimes physical resemblance is enough, sometimes it's usage, and sometimes it's something else entirely.

The conclusion to this question of resemblance is that depending on the intention of the moment, the same sequence of patterns will not always be labeled or identified as belonging to the same category. The same tactical pattern can therefore be more or less analogous to many others, meaning it can be categorized in various ways, with other factors like intention or context determining which label is most appropriate at that moment.

Emmanuel Sander and Douglas Hofstadter, in their work on the role of analogy in cognition, relate this question of belonging to multiple categories to the complexity of the world:

> "The everyday concepts *band*, *chair*, *teapot*, *mess*, and *letter 'A'* are very different from specialized notions such as *prime number* or *DNA*. The latter also have unimaginably many members, but what is shared by all their members is expressible precisely and unambiguously. By contrast, in the mental structure underpinning a word like "band," "chair," "mess" or "teapot" there lurks a boundless, blurry richness that is completely passed over by dictionaries, because spelling out such subtleties is not a dictionary's aim."[1]

We don't realize how much even mundane actions, like descending a staircase without thinking, or

1. Douglas Hofstadter and Emmanuel Sander, *Surfaces and Essences: Analogy as the Fuel and Fire of* Thinking (New York: Basic Books, 2013).

grasping a cup from a table, involve working with highly flexible categories. To grab an object efficiently, I must not only recognize it and identify its position in the surrounding space. I must also anticipate. Within the larger action plan of extending my arm and grasping the cup, I must integrate the specificity of the cup before me, the type of grip I'll need to use to grab it, and ensure my hand forms the shape of the object before I even touch it.

Analyzing, understanding, anticipating, forecasting—managing tactical patterns makes it possible, allows it, and for that reason, I believe it is the mechanism at the heart of intelligence; it *is* intelligence.

Faced with the evolving scales of threat, the human brain has hardly evolved over the last thousands of years. It has been gradually built, structured, and adapted over tens of millions of years, long before the historical period. Thanks to its plasticity, it has used its cognitive apparatus, developed to analyze things that move and evolve over time, to recognize faces, and applied it to understanding books, writings, paintings, screens—allowing it to extend its sensitivity to the tactical processes running through the universe. Organic AI is the next phase in this long history. It will allow us to multiply our ability to intuit an increasingly complex world. But before we discuss the consequences it will have on our lives, we must first consider the technical approach to its possibilities.

7. How to summarize what intelligence is

A system capable of "managing" tactical patterns would be perceived as intelligent!

Managing tactical patterns means perceiving situational developments, recording them, and if a similar pattern has already been recorded, evolving it to retain only the common aspects of both, gradually refining it over time to capture its essence.

Managing tactical patterns also involves knowing how to retrieve future steps of a similar recorded pattern to compare it with what is currently being perceived, as from the start of this paragraph, we are already in the future.

Managing tactical patterns further involves dealing with them on different scales of detail and timeframes.

It also includes handling tactical patterns triggered by and sensitive to the co-occurrence of simultaneous events.

Finally, managing reversible tactical patterns involves breaking down high-level actions (like hitting a target with an arrow) into basic, microscopic sequences of actions for each relevant muscle fiber.

Such a system would be perceived as an intelligent system, would be inseparable from an intelligent system; and would be an intelligent system.

I believe that this is what we call intelligence, and that this is how it functions.

4

MAKING ARTIFICIAL INTELLIGENCE INTELLIGENT

Drawing inspiration from the brain to create artificial intelligence involves transforming this patchwork of observations, scientific publications, intuitions, and convictions into a model, that is, an architecture of algorithms. While the elements presented in the earlier chapters of this book provide an interesting and unique perspective on how intelligence and the cortex function, they don't, on their own, provide a ready-to-go model for computer science applications.

Our dual-path approach led to the development of this coherent model, aligned with the concepts from the book's early chapters: a "bottom-up" process, similar to that of someone doing a puzzle, feeling their way and testing ideas until pieces—and eventually larger sections of the final model—emerge from the chaos. And a "top-down" process that begins with the desired global architecture and gradually refines it until a set of functions can be articulated to implement it. When these two research paths converge—when the model becomes sufficiently precise to guide the trial-and-error process, which in turn refines the model—a major milestone is achieved. This is what happened at AnotherBrain in early 2024.

The bottom-up process involved exploring the initial works of Patrick Pirim, which were strongly inspired by the local workings of the micro-columns and leading up to industrial applications. Patrick is an electronics engineer who, early on, chose to draw inspiration from nature. One of his first projects was with a large French industrial electronics supplier, responding to a bid to control a robotic arm designed to pick up items from a conveyor belt. This was over forty years ago. The focus was on item orientation: since the items needed to be grasped differently depending on their orientation, the system had to detect how the items were presented. Of course, the competitors responded with early image processing solutions, thus programming and information technology, whereas Patrick was an electronics engineer without access to the same kind of knowledge. He chose a very unique approach, one that would accompany him throughout his career: he asked his network of experts in "how does nature do it?"—neuroscientists, doctors, biologists, and specialists from the Collège de France—how nature determined orientation in things. He then built an integrated circuit, a chip that carried out what he had discovered. And he won the bid. As in many other projects that followed, refining his integrated circuits to meet new challenges, each time learning how nature would proceed faced with these new questions. These included applications like discriminating video streams in a bid to improve prison surveillance systems in France, or counting the number of people in the crowded buses of Shanghai, among many others. Each time, he improved his circuits based on what he had understood about how nature worked; each time for industrial problems where clients were not friends who wanted to help him, but professionals who wanted it *to work* in a cost-effective way, and who compared his response with that of competitors.

All the applications involved industrial image processing, and gradually, Patrick Pirim's chip came closer to the functioning of the cortical micro-columns of the visual area—closer to the workings of all the micro-columns in the cortex. There was still work to do to finalize this resemblance and then generalize it to other micro-columns, especially to understand the connections and relationships between them, but there was already a powerful foundation in place.

We continued down this path, attempting to solve simple problems, chosen as stepping stones toward the development of an artificial cortex or met industrial needs that could ideally fund our research. This process involved the development and refinement of algorithms through trial and error, while drawing inspiration from our understanding of the senses and the cortex.

However, this approach, akin to an evolutionary process driven by *blind* local improvements, exploring ways to calculate seeking a local optimum, doesn't lead to paradigm shifts or address the global optimum that is Organic AI. Therefore, it didn't necessarily align with the goal of creating a global artificial intelligence whose definition, by the way, remained quite unclear. We needed a global model.

On the other hand, the top-down approach, which aims to describe this global model, gained substance as an early model emerged from our research, particularly from our understanding of tactical patterns—consistent with our bottom-up explorations. Once this loop was closed, meaning when the emerging global model was sufficiently coherent with our trial-and-error efforts, a bidirectional progression could be set in motion, with dual criteria for success: solving the selected problems and the clearer perspective of contributing to the functioning of an intelligence.

In all, the top-down approach ensures the overall coherence of a system behaving like intelligence by defining objectives and structures that direct the local optimizations carried out by the bottom-up approach. This guarantees that each part of the model contributes effectively to the global intelligence.

This is the model I will now present: *our* translation of how intelligence works into a set of interrelated functions. It paves the way for implementations of AI that function like the brain. This is what we are doing at AnotherBrain: a continuous loop between improving the model, refining its implementation over time, and enriching it with scientific publications and expert meetings to fill gaps or explore together. It is a common research method that we apply to our own model.

From now on, whenever I describe what cortical maps do, or any element of the cortex, I will refer to our interpretation within the framework of our model.

Disclaimer: The model is not complete as of this writing, in mid-September 2024. Not because it presents inconsistencies that need addressing, but simply because it does not yet integrate some necessary functions. We know how to approach them, but they have not yet been implemented. We have a sufficiently clear understanding, with enough results, to consider that the backbone of the model is robust and forms the framework for this sought-after Organic AI. With enough results to envision a demonstrator that will prove the relevance and power of our approach. With a sufficient base of results to expand team sizes, broaden and complete the model, its implementations, and early applications, thus accelerating progress—while remaining unified by this backbone to avoid the centrifugal drift that could arise from the multiplication of leaderships and scientific visions that would confuse us along the way. And with enough results to convince others of our approach, particularly in order to raise the necessary funds to finance this acceleration.

1. Let's dive into the description of the organic AI model

To give a guiding thread to this chapter, I will summarize our understanding of the cortex in broad strokes as follows:

The functioning of intelligence is based on a network of cortical maps, each analyzing a receptive field made up of one or more streams of configurations. Each map produces a flow of labels, semantically describing what happened in its receiving field, in accordance with the analysis time constant. All maps are agnostic—they function the same way and are specialized only according to the streams that feed them.

All flows circulate in both directions, from the analytical (details) to the semantic, with increasingly abstract concepts, meaning richer labels, and vice versa; this allows the reconstruction of details from semantic labels.

To do this, each map begins by identifying everything significant in its receptive field, which we translate as a list of descriptors that constitute the signature of what is in the receptive field.

Then it labels this signature by searching in its memory for the labels whose characteristics best match the perceived signature (it's as if each map has its own label memory) and produces an output flow of labels referenced in the flow, meaning characterized and positioned, which can then be the input for a higher-level cortical map.

Simultaneously, after the labeling, the so-called memory of the map is slightly modified to integrate the new experience, which constitutes learning.

All of this will be clarified, and I will structure the description of our model according to the following breakdown: cortical maps and incoming flows, descriptors and signatures, labeling, and learning.

2. Cortical maps and incoming flows

A cortical map handles a receptive field analyzed according to an integration time—or, more prosaically, it handles a subject: vision when the receptive field is the entire visual field of the retina, hearing when the receptive field is the entire auditory field of the cochlea, for lower-level maps (closer to inputs/ outputs), or, for higher-level maps, animals, for example, with a receptive field composed of a combination of visual, auditory, olfactory label flows…

Each one is composed of micro-columns and columns functioning identically. Together, they form the network of maps. It is the structure of this network of cortical maps—i.e., the relationships between them, their topology—that creates intelligence. Each map takes as input the outputs/results from other maps or information or inputs from the outside world. Each map has an integration time that increases as abstraction rises, i.e., with the scale of integrated elements, the richness of labels. Together, they cover the cortex's surface in proportion to their usage, most likely in line with their demand.

The articulation of these maps can be calculated in different ways:

Deterministically to solve a particular problem.

Emergently, from a set of input streams to optimize predefined criteria or based on regular feedback.

Biologically inspired, attempting to reproduce biological models for study and experimentation.

If one wants to give real intelligence to a robot vacuum, for example—which is quite effective, although there is still room for improvement if you don't want to find your robot stuck on the wire of the halogen lamp or on the table leg every third day—it doesn't need many cortical maps. Four or five maps, with "manually" determined connections and parameters, will suffice. "Visual," sensory, motor and integration cards—they'll all be the same, of course, but I'm naming them according to the sensors/actuators to which they'll be connected, to make it more meaningful (presumably, one of each will suffice).

For simple problems like these, as well as more complex problems—such as autonomous vehicles, where suppliers aim to control the entire operational chain—we will need to define the precise articulation of the system's components. A manufacturer of fully autonomous vehicles, for instance, would never want the intelligence of the driving system to develop unpredictably from accumulated driving experiences without being fully mastered. Instead, they would likely allow the intelligence to emerge organically from driving experiences and the structuring of cortical maps, but ultimately intervene to manually refine and fully control the system's articulation.

But for more open-ended or evolving subjects, where all situations aren't known, the organization of the map network must emerge from the experiences the system undergoes. An exhaustive network whose links strengthen or weaken depending on usage is one approach, but other methods based on dynamic attractors, in a sense self-directed, and more economical in experience usage, offer alternatives. I will speak more about this later.

Finally, one might want to replicate the functioning of human intelligence for experimental and research purposes or to draw inspiration from it for specific applications by reproducing the structure of the cortical maps in a human brain (which contains around 400 of them). Yves and Nikki Burnod, researchers at CNRS and INSERM, undertook a project in *The Panoramic Brain* to map out the most complex cognitive loops—those involved in learning and the use of our highest cognitive abilities[1]. They identified seven loops of cortical maps, the seven rings of competence (the vital skills ring, the social skills ring, the motor skills ring, the vocal skills ring, the verbal skills ring, the imagination ring, and finally, the mental control ring), together forming what they call the "atlas of competencies." Their work provides key insights into reproducing the articulation of the cortical maps of a human brain.

Solving a specific problem with real intelligence, like a robot vacuum or drones, does not require as many cortical maps as human intelligence, even though the underlying mechanisms are the same. This means it is already possible to validate the principles and functioning of Organic AI without having to fully recreate human-like intelligence. The key here is ensuring that the mechanics of a cortical map function properly, that its output can serve as the input for another, and that a single map can take in multiple outputs from other maps—processing multiple concurrent data streams unfolding at the same time.

3. How are the input streams of cortical maps structured?

In the visual area, we could almost describe it as a flow of images, or essentially, two-dimensional "matrices," a sort of video feed entering the primary

1. *The Panoramic Brain, op. cit.*

cortical map. But this is just an illustration, because in reality, the visual system behaves as if the pixels at the center of the image are smaller, more densely packed, and in color, while those at the periphery are much larger, more sensitive, less dense, and in black and white. Yes, you read that right: outside the tiny area of the fovea—which covers about the size of a two-euro coin held at arm's length—our vision is actually quite blurry, primarily in black and white, but highly sensitive. This explains the saying "At night, all cats are gray," since in low light, we essentially see in black and white. In a sense, this setup is comparable to a distorted grid, making it somewhat equivalent to a two-dimensional matrix. Only somewhat, though, because the actual optical input doesn't capture static intensity values "per pixel" across the entire field of view—it only records variations and changes in the perceived image over time. However, this doesn't affect our overall model.

A similar principle applies to the cortical map of the tactile field, which processes sensations from the skin. It's as if a grid were laid over the skin, but with highly uneven mesh sizes—extremely dense and precise at the fingertips and around the mouth, nearly nonexistent in the middle of the back, with each grid cell containing a sensor whose value changes over time. In fact, the similarity to the visual system is even stronger than one might think, since in fact, skin contains multiple types of receptors—for pressure, temperature, humidity, superficial cuts, deep cuts, and more. Each of these sensitivities is mapped onto a different type of grid, making a striking parallel with color versus black-and-white vision. These grids, with their varying mesh sizes, are analyzed by cortical columns, which divide up the irregular grid cells, each handling different-sized sensory fields. Once again, input to the map of skin sensitivity functions in a similar way to an flow of two-dimensional matrices.

When looking at the olfactory analysis map, we find something intriguing: the olfactory system appears to project perceived smells onto the olfactory bulb—a specialized brain structure—before the signals reach the cortex. This projection happens in two dimensions, with carbon chain length on one axis and the chemical family (esters, alcohols, aldehydes, etc.) on the other. Again, a stream of two-dimensional matrices. One of the key studies that inferred this spatial projection of smells in the olfactory bulb was conducted by Richard Axel and Linda Buck, whose work earned them the 2004 Nobel Prize in Medicine.[2]

It feels less natural to think of the audio input as a stream of two-dimensional matrices since each ear seems like a simple microphone recording variations in intensity over time. This would lead us to view it as two separate time-based streams for two separate points. But once again, things are not as they seem. Each cochlea, the actual sound receptor in the ear, is made up of 3,500 internal vibratory cilia—the internal hair cells—which act like tiny microphones, each tuned to a specific frequency band. Each of these cells functions as a band-pass filter, and together,

2. Linda Buck and Richard Axel, "A Novel Multigene Family May Encode Odorant Receptors: A Molecular Basis for Odor Recognition," *Cell* 65, no. 1 (1991): 175-87.

they perform the equivalent of a Fourier transform on incoming sound—breaking it down by intensity across different frequency ranges. You can visualize this by looking at a sonogram, which represents how this frequency decomposition evolves over time (with frequency displayed on the vertical axis in the image below).

Fig. 9: Sonogram: song of a bluebird. Source: Wikipedia.
The abscissa represents time (ms), and the ordinate represents frequency (Hz).

Moreover, hearing relies on two ears spaced about fifteen centimeters apart. Each ear detects sound that has traveled slowly through the air at around 330 meters per second. Because of this, each ear receives a slightly different sound; or rather, both receive the same sound, but slightly out of sync: the ear closer to the sound source picks up the signal a tiny bit earlier than the other. The slow speed of sound propagation through the air makes this difference perceptible to the ear, which results in a difference in the phase of the received signal. Therefore, the phase of the signal is not the same in both ears, depending on the lateralization of the sound source. We can then analyze the sound flow as if it were placed on a grid, where the horizontal axis is the phase of the signal, and thus its lateralization, while the vertical axis represents its intensity as a function of frequency.

However, there's a more useful approach: think of the "sound image" as a two-dimensional matrix. This "sonogram in the period" represents the changes in sound intensity over time for each frequency. Essentially, it captures a snapshot of the sound's evolution during each cycle, which is especially useful for analyzing periodic sounds. For example, if a sound has a fundamental frequency of G2 at 98 hertz, typical of a male voice, the period chosen to capture the sonogram will be approximately 1/100th of a second, or 10 milliseconds. However, if this fundamental frequency is A3, typical of a female voice, the sonogram will be captured every 4.5 milliseconds. If you adjust the sonogram's image within each cycle, stretching or shrinking it so that it always spans the same width, you create a representation of the sound that's independent of its fundamental frequency. For instance, when you say the letter "a," the "sonogram in the period" will look the same whether you say it in a high or low pitch!

In sound perception, the signal's period is usually represented on the vertical axis rather than its frequency. However, since the period is just the inverse of frequency, this doesn't change the overall reasoning. In fact, it is quite natural to consider sound as a flow of two-dimensional matrices.

By generalizing these observations, and based on the results of Mountcastle and of Hubel and Wiesel, who noted the deep homogeneity of the cortex (you will often read this phrase), we consider, *in our model,* that all the inputs to cortical maps, and therefore all the pattern flows, are flows of two-dimensional matrices. Each cortical map thus receives one or more flows of two-dimensional matrices, of which it analyzes a slice, that is, a batch of a certain number of consecutive two-dimensional matrices, with the number corresponding to its integration time, and describes what is most characteristic in this slice—which means labeling it—then produces an output flow of two-dimensional matrices in which the found labels are positioned.

4. DESCRIPTORS

Let's now get into the heart of the reactor.

What a cortical map first does is extract the most significant characteristics from incoming flows. So, it generates from the incoming matrix flows what is called the signature of everything they contain. To do this, a group of automata analyzes different aspects of the signals along different axes and finds characteristic configurations, which it transforms into descriptors; the signature is the set of characterized descriptors, with their positioning in the flow.

Now, let's go into detail, and for this, I will approach this step by step, starting with something simple, which I will enrich until we get the big picture.

I will again illustrate these analyses using the example of vision, which is more intuitive and easier to grasp, but they apply more generally and in the same way to any signal or combination of signals represented as flows of two-dimensional matrices evolving over time.

5. Imagine a cortical vision map looking —that is, analyzing, since all the unfolding of cortical maps is mechanical, automatic, inevitable—a simple image of a black square on a light background

The map does two things in parallel: it focuses on attention points, particular points that stand out from the rest, for local analysis; and it searches for the contours of homogeneous areas, such as for our square, areas of the same color, for a global analysis of the shape.

The attention points, or "salient points," are those that stand out from the background in some way. These could be a distinct color spot, a sharp contrast, an angle, movement compared to the surrounding area, or a more noticeable curve (a smaller radius), thus more accentuated… We know about saccadic eye movements, through which our eyes jump three times per second from one point to another, sweeping the scene that unfolds before us; it's the same mechanism, with the eyes moving from attention point to attention point, without us being aware of it. Analyzing only what's worth analyzing and with each saccade, performing a very local but therefore precise analysis. Well, there are equivalent mechanisms for other modalities, such as sound, which allow the maps to analyze successively and precisely several very focused areas, several reduced receptive fields, and find a sequence of signatures, a succession of patterns.

Regarding contour analysis, in our implementation, the map retrieves the angle of orientation of the edge (its tangent) and its curvature. If several shapes have disjointed contours, even nested one inside the other, they will be treated separately.

Then, for each contour, the map looks for the contiguous pixels with the same curvature and those with the same tangent. Each zone of contiguous pixels with the same tangent, say with homogeneous values, represents a segment of the edge that is a straight line, and each area with homogeneous curvature represents an arc of a circle (which allows us to approximate the shape of a curved edge by a succession of small osculating arcs—those that "fit the curve as closely as possible" at each point). Finally, the junctions between two of these areas represent angles.

Each element can be described in specific ways: straight line segments are characterized by their length, orientation, and center position; circular arcs by their radius, angular size, center, and orientation; and angles by their angle size, center, and orientation.

We've found our first contour descriptors!

It is clear that this description is not unique. For example, one could replace a straight segment with two segments half the length, but it still allows us to characterize a given shape. For instance, four right angles and four segments of equal length, oriented at 90° to each other, and positioned in the correct way, form our square.

We notice, regarding these descriptors, information of several kinds: the *what*, the *where*, and the *how*. An arc of a circle with a 90° opening—thus a quarter circle—of a certain radius is a *what*, just like a straight segment of a certain length or a 90° angle.

The *where* refers to the positioning of the descriptor within the shape and thus to its coordinates in a reference frame related to the shape: there is a right angle at this position. Finally, the *how* refers to the way in which the descriptor is perceived: its orientation, its size, and even its left-right symmetry. The first time a shape is perceived, the reference frame assigned to it is a natural reference frame—the center of gravity and horizontal and vertical axes—but we will see, for a shape that has been perceived many times and memorized, that this reference frame will gradually evolve into an object-reference frame of the shape, in the sense that it will be the one in which the shape is most frequently perceived, equivalent to a 3D frame. The reference frame of a giraffe will have its vertical axis in the direction of height, so its largest dimension will be oriented vertically; while that of a crocodile, on the other hand, will have its largest dimension oriented horizontally.

This reference frame is directly linked to Jeff Hawkins's thesis in his book *A Thousand Brains*, where he discusses the need for a reference frame tied to each "object," a sort of grid attached to the object that allows for the precise positioning of its characteristic elements, its descriptors. His example, taken from the tactile domain, is as follows: he refers to the experience of holding a mug in your hand and being able to identify it as a mug without even looking at it, because our fingers touch a smooth, cylindrical, cold shape, which our cortex has recognized as one of many possible forms (a glass, a bottle...). But by moving our fingers over the object and thus shifting our attention within the object's reference frame, at some point, we touch a rounded edge, and as we continue moving, we detect a handle… which gradually allows us to distinguish, amongst the candidates, the object that exhibits the right descriptors in the right locations. This mechanism is very similar to the saccadic eye movements, rapid eye movements followed by pauses to analyze, called the "scanpath" and shows the close interconnection between perception and action: there is no perception without action.

Our GDS model, in this regard, is consistent with Jeff Hawkins's theories on intelligence and the brain and appears to be a way of implementing them. Although it is much earlier, since the notions of *where* and *what,* intrinsic to the implementation of the dynamic attractor, have been used in GDS documents for at least twenty years (the first patent for the dynamic attractor was filed in 1987).

We also found our first content descriptor: the interior of the shape is, by definition, homogeneous, because it is through the homogeneity of its content that we determined its contour, and it can be characterized here by its black color. And if the black square does not move, there is no movement descriptor: we now have our first signature, that of a shape whose contour is defined by four straight segments of equal length and four right angles oriented at 90° to each other, and whose interior is filled with black.

This extreme simplification already raises important questions. *Why choose tangent, curvature, and color as description criteria? Isn't this choice of analysis axes restrictive? Isn't it overly tied to vision?*

6. Analysis axes: GDS

The descriptors detect and encode what is in the two-dimensional matrix flows, the discontinuities, the homogeneities, the evolutions. Many types of descriptors could be imagined for this, a whole bunch, or let them emerge like with Deep Learning (using large amounts of data for that purpose). However, based on the work of Hubel and Wiesel on micro-columns, we chose to limit ourselves to the GDS criteria—Global, Dynamic, and Structural—which seem to be the axes that nature has chosen to analyze everything that happens to a living organism.

The Global criterion focuses on the signal's intensity, identifying areas where the intensity is roughly constant and uniform. I have italicized the word because it concerns the intensity of the signal within the two-dimensional matrix. For vision, this could be the intensity of brightness or the intensity of each color, so the overall color. But more judiciously and more generally, we could talk about the energy of the signal. The Global criterion thus refers to the energy in the signal and characterizes zones whose energy is homogeneous.

The Dynamic criterion, similarly, identifies areas where the signal's change over time is consistent. It looks at how the signal evolves over time (its temporal derivative). This could involve detecting the direction of movement or the speed of change in the signal. It looks at the temporal derivative of the signal, *d/dt*. This could be the direction of evolution for a moving zone, for example, or the intensity of the variation, thus the speed of evolution.

The Dynamic criterion thus refers to the evolution of the signal over time and characterizes areas whose evolution is homogeneous.

Lastly, the Structural criterion focuses on identifying areas where the signal's spatial variation is consistent. For two adjacent points, it examines how the signal changes vertically compared to horizontally (its spatial derivative, *dy/dx*), essentially measuring how the signal's shape varies across the space. When points on the edge of an area, for example, have the same spatial derivative, they are aligned in the same direction. When points on the edge of an area have derivatives *that vary by the same amount* from one point to the next, they are on a curve with constant curvature, an arc of a circle. The Structural criterion thus refers to the structure, the form of the signal on the two-dimensional matrix, and characterizes areas that locally exhibit a homogeneous form.

It is important to note that these analysis axes were chosen by us, as opposed to those of Deep Learning, which emerge from massive datasets and may *a priori* seem less interesting. However, these are the axes that nature has selected as being the most pertinent, on average, to analyzing data of the type that nature needs to process, meaning continuous spatiotemporal variation data; data that evolves progressively over time and moves progressively, not jumping from one position to another without passing through the middle. In short, everything we experience.

Our choice of GDS criteria is justified by the search for consistency with natural processes, which should optimize the effectiveness of our AI in environments that reflect real-world conditions. Our artificial intelligence system will, *a priori,* not be able to handle data and situations outside of what exists in our real world, so it will not always be good or suited for data analytics, which may need to handle discontinuous data, but it will be highly optimized for everything else.

We could summarize this formulation by saying that the flow of two-dimensional matrices is analyzed according to the intensity of the pixels in the two-dimensional matrices (Global), their temporal evolutions or variations (Dynamic), and their spatial variations (Structural). For each of these analyses, we search for areas of the same values and specify their characteristics.

7. How to find and characterize descriptors?

We have several approaches for finding descriptors (our research process always explores multiple paths in parallel): a "brute force," computational, and deterministic approach; an emerging, nature-inspired approach; and a target approach, which is the generalization of the emerging approach. This is the one I will describe, although it is not yet fully implemented (the first approach, already implemented, validated the philosophy of the descriptors).

This process uses "dynamic attractors" (DAs), a simple mathematical tool that is applied to each cell in a two-dimensional matrix representing the receptive field. These attractors are designed to identify and converge on the largest contiguous area where a specific criterion—such as the speed of evolution—remains consistent. For example, in the case of speed, the attractors would locate the largest area within the receptive field where the cells evolve at roughly the same speed. If a plane passes through the visual field, even in front of a cloudy background, its pixels will be classified as having the same speed of evolution. These dynamic attractors make it possible to find contiguous areas of the receptive field that behave homogenously according to the analyzed criteria. This approach has been used industrially since 1988 in a variant involving several integrated circuits and has demonstrated its great effectiveness.

An inhibitory input completes each attractor, allowing other DAs to disregard the structure already found, so they don't converge to the same area. Thus, a group of four attractors, for example, can automatically find the four most important zones where the chosen criterion is homogeneous and automatically characterize them in the process. It doesn't matter what the criterion is, or what data flow is being processed.

One can take it a step further: rather than assigning four DAs to the "evolution speed" analysis axis, five others to the "texture" axis, etc., one can create a bank of several dynamic attractors, "recruitable" automatically by the GDS analyzers that need them, for example, based on the energy of the descriptors. All GDS analysis criteria, all of them, are then exposed to the bank of DAs, which will gradually assign themselves to all descriptors from the most important to the least important. They will automatically detect and refine the most characteristic descriptors, as many as there are DAs in the bank.

The list of descriptors perceived in the two-dimensional matrix flow will thus result from what is most characteristic of this specific flow analyzed according to the pre-chosen G, D, and S axes: what changes the fastest, the strongest curvatures, the strongest value variations (we would say *contrast*, in the context of vision). The analysis by this DA bank reveals what is most significant and characterizes it with descriptors.

8. Analysis from the general to the specific: squinting to see better

But that's not all: finding the outline of a shape is like measuring the length of the coastline of Brittany—to reference Benoît Mandelbrot's introduction to fractals. If you measure the length of the Breton coast with a rigid wooden ruler one meter long, following the coast's edge closely, you'll get a certain value. If your ruler is ten centimeters long, you'll enter the recesses that you previously skipped over, and you'll find the length is greater. If your ruler measures one centimeter, you'll enter even more recesses, yielding a still greater length. One millimeter: even more. And so on.

So, what exactly does the "length of the Breton coastline" mean? Does this question even make sense? It's a fractal curve, and this is how the mathematical concept of fractals was introduced by Benoît Mandelbrot.

In the case of real-world objects, nothing is simple: there are no areas of uniform color in the real world, there is always texture, granularity—even in the uniform white color of your living room wall. There are no perfectly straight lines or regular arcs either. There are always imperfections. There is nothing in the perceptual field of an organism that remains still, as the organism itself is in motion. So, there is always texture, movement, imperfections, and finding the contour of a shape is a puzzle.

Think of your wooden coffee table, whose cortical vision map tries to characterize its shape. You see the table, but also the grain of the wood, which delimits "sub-zones" within it. And, if your living room floor is made of wood with a similar hue, why stop at one point in the image to define the table's contour? Isolating a textured and colored shape against a background that is itself textured and colored is not easy in many situations. Often, a combination of modalities (movement, distance, color, texture…) is needed. But each must contribute and be perceived at the right level of detail.

So, we—and we believe the brain does as well—have chosen to analyze from the general to the specific, from the global phenomenon down to its details, stopping the analysis when enough information has been gathered. It's a bit like squinting your eyes to better see an overall shape without being distracted by textures and small details that interfere with the "reading" of a phenomenon. This multiscale analysis allows the automatic selection of the scales that carry the relevant information.

To do this, we start by blurring the image before conducting the GDS analyses. The more precise term here is the application of a low-pass filter—spatial for analyzing the two-dimensional matrix, temporal for analyzing the time flow—which only shows the large structures, the major shapes, and filters out the details. Then, we extract the signature from it. Finally, we perform multiple GDS analyses: one on a heavily filtered image, one on an intermediate filtering to refine the analysis, and, for example, one last on the original, most precise image. A simple way to achieve this filtering is by reducing the image size, but this is just an operational method; we perform three levels of filtering because it suffices for most standard-sized images/matrices. But for larger images, like those from much higher-resolution sensors, this number will need to be increased.

At a given level of blur, each pixel becomes an average of all its surrounding pixels, with the extent of averaging depending on the strength of the blur. By analyzing the contours of shapes in this blurred image, we can identify regions that are homogeneous—where the texture's characteristic size is smaller than the blur factor. At the strongest blur level, you can find uniform areas that correspond to areas of less blurring, but also to uniform areas with a repeated uniformity: a texture with a characteristic dimension smaller than the blur. At a strong level of blur, even a brightly colored tartan will merge into a uniform area, and with less blurring, we can begin to detect the structure of the tartan.

This multiscale analysis thus returns three signatures: one at each scale, but corresponding to the same perceived shape. This makes it possible to clarify some ambiguous descriptors at one scale by analyzing what they correspond to at another scale—what we call "error correction"—but above all, to select the most relevant signature among the three, depending on the subject being analyzed. When you look at a tree, are you interested in its overall shape or the shape of its leaves?

Finally, this method allows us to define the contour and characterize the "textures" of an area: at the most blurred scale, what was perceived as a textured area (for example, the grain of wood in a parquet floor or a wooden table) becomes a roughly uniform area of average color. However, this area is supposed to cover the same location as at a slightly less blurred scale, which enables us to identify subtle nuances, even colors, and entirely different structures at the less blurred scale, but that still belong to the same textured area.

At the same time, the contour of the area is refined. And again, at the original base scale. This allows us to conclude that such an area, presenting different colors and structures (for example, broad parallel lines alternating between light brown and yellowish brown, spaced roughly evenly, or a checkerboard pattern of black and white squares, or a vertical alternating pattern of black and white stripes…) is a textured zone whose texture has been characterized, and whose contour has been clarified.

9. THE IMPORTANCE OF CONTOURS IN IDENTIFYING A SHAPE: COMBINING CRITÈRIA

The shape, typically represented by its outline or perimeter, is a fundamental element in identifying perceived objects. But it is not always accessible, due to obstructions or blending with the background. For example, recognizing a voice among a crowd when multiple people speak at the same time; a termite-eating beetle that shares the same scent as its prey; or a Uroplatus gecko camouflaged on a tree, as shown in Figure 10 below—it's challenging to discern the shape's outline, making it difficult to recognize the animal until it moves!

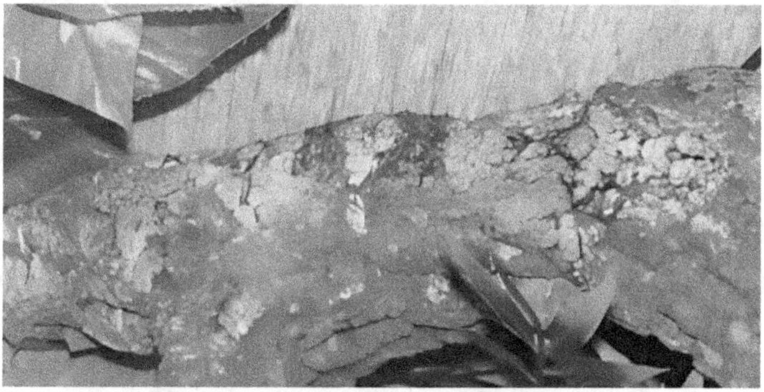

Fig. 10: *Uroplatus* gecko hidden in a tree (https://fr.m.wikipedia.org/wiki/Fichier:Gekkoninae_Uroplatus_sikorae_camouflage_horiz.png).

To identify shapes, we must combine multiple criteria: color uniformity, texture, motion, or distance via binocular vision… Each of these factors reinforces the ability to detect the shape's outline for analysis. As soon as the gecko moves, its shape becomes visible.

None of these criteria alone is sufficient to characterize a shape, but their combination significantly improves our ability to identify it. However, this approach doesn't always work; we cannot always recognize the shape of something in front of us unless something triggers our awareness. Nature, in an effort to protect prey from predators or, conversely, to assist predators in approaching their targets stealthily, manipulates these criteria to complicate shape identification. This phenomenon is known as camouflage, which can be visual, auditory, or olfactory.

Regarding shape detection through the combination of G, D, and S analyses described earlier—performed in our model at the input of the descriptor detection algorithm—I experienced immense joy when I discovered, after developing this mechanism "from scratch," that layer four of the micro-columns contained sub-layers that performed the same analyses and combined them to improve shape detection. Immense joy in the *a posteriori* validation of a thought like, "For this to work, it must necessarily work like this." I derive personal and intimate delight from this, as this result, perhaps known to everyone for a long time, was felt as validation for me, someone who didn't know about these sub-layers in the fourth layer.

Another parallel between our descriptors and how nature works is shown by Doris Tsao's study on face recognition. In studying facial recognition in macaques, Doris Tsao demonstrated that it relied on twenty-five shape criteria and twenty-five "content" criteria. In other words, fifty criteria are *sufficient* to identify a person, thus labeling a face. More importantly for our discussion, the criteria to which she converged, the descriptors, are: shape = contours, and content.[3]

---

3. Doris Tsao, "Functional compartmentalization and viewpoint generalization within the macaque face-processing system," *Science* 330, no. 6005 (2010), p. 845–851.

10. Too many details kill understanding: categorizing descriptors

At this stage, we are able to precisely identify the contours of significant areas and define a signature that describes them well enough to regenerate them if desired. However, too much precision, too many details, can hinder understanding. Just as it would be difficult to explain a Monet painting by describing every tiny variation in color of the Impressionist's brushstrokes, or to guide you to the nearest subway station by detailing every minor curve of the boulevard you are following, it is often easier and more effective to understand a description by focusing on its main characteristics, its broader picture. Of course, this comes with a loss of information—but if it's more efficient? Is that *acceptable*, or not? Let's see.

A good way to address this issue is to categorize descriptors, grouping them by similarity. For example, we could decide that all angles between 85° and 95° are considered right angles, meaning that an approximately right angle would simply be treated as a right angle.

Of course, if you are a mathematician or an engineer, this might be problematic. But in everyday life, it can greatly simplify descriptions.

One possible approach is to define nine angle categories: 0°, 30°, 45°, 60°, 90°, 120°, 135°, 150°, and 180°, using the closest one to characterize any given angle (the number 9 is arbitrary, just for illustration). In this way, "30°" is no longer a precise angle but a category of angles roughly around 30°. Each angle category is identified by a label, such as "label 30°" in the above example, but for generalization purposes, it can be seen as a letter in an alphabet of angles. If we define nine angle labels, then this alphabet consists of nine letters (though we could just as easily choose fifteen or twenty). The signature of a shape's angles then becomes a word composed of several letters, each representing an approximate angle. A shape with angles of 89°, 95°, 90°, and 87° would thus be described as having four "right" angles—or rather, four "letters" representing right angles. This idea of an alphabet for each type of label, with as many letters as there are possible labels for a given axis of analysis, is very generic.

We could create several "alphabets" for different types of descriptors: one for angles, one for straight lines, one for arcs, and one for textures. To illustrate, imagine these "alphabets" as being similar to Latin, Greek, Arabic, or Phoenician alphabets. Each "word" we construct would be a mix of letters from these various alphabets, with each letter representing a distinct descriptor. While this method won't give a precise reconstruction of the shape, it offers an efficient way to describe the perceived object in broad terms, which is often enough for most purposes. Reconstructing the perceived shape would be less precise but likely *sufficient*—and much more efficient.

Of course, this categorization of descriptors, grouping them by similarity under a single "name" or "letter of the right alphabet," is nothing more than labeling—assigning a code to a group of entities. In this chapter, we are dealing with labels for descriptors, since we are converting them into semantic labels, or letters. Later, we will categorize configurations (patterns) and then sequences of configurations, creating labels for patterns and for sequences of patterns.

I have deliberately used terms like *sufficient*, *acceptable*, and *understandable* several times because, as previously mentioned, excessive detail hinders comprehension—while too little detail does the same! Should we seek the right balance in descriptor categorization to ensure that simplifying labeling remains effective? Several mechanisms could be employed for this, ranging from a simple equal-distribution method to emergent mechanisms that enable labels and descriptors to evolve based on the specific needs of the map.

As a starting point for reflection, consider edge detection in the visual cortex. Hubel and Wiesel showed that the micro-columns in the V1 visual area responded preferentially to specific edge orientations, with adjacent micro-columns responding to angles that differ by 16° to 18°. This 16° to 18° step between labels—essentially the "letters" in the brain's V1 area—was later refined in studies such as the one by Blasdel and Salama in 1986[4].

The descriptors of the cortex indeed appear to be categorized and encoded in the form I have referred to as "letters," and in the case of orientations, the cortex would use ten or eleven letters (depending on whether we consider steps of 16° or 18°).

---

4. Gary G. Blasdel and Guy Salama, "Voltage-Sensitive Dyes Reveal a Modular Organization in Monkey Striate Cortex," *Nature* 321 (1986): 579-85.

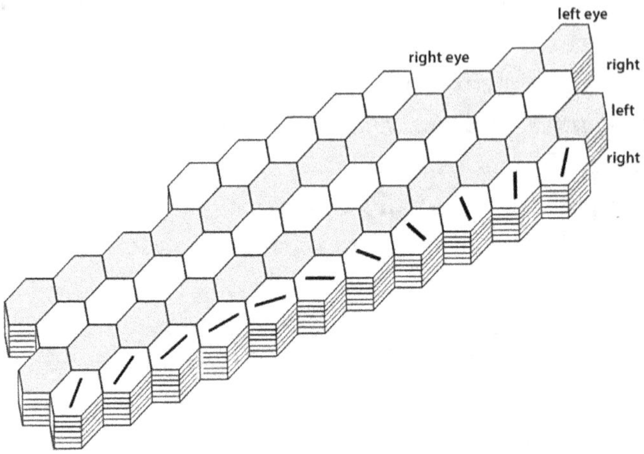

Fig. 11: S Diagram of the structuring of a column and its micro-columns in the striate cortex of the monkey (Hubel 1994).

The categorization of descriptors in neuroscience corresponds to synaptic codes, those synaptic vectors determined by the tuning curves of neurons. One of the remarkable properties of cortical columns is the regularity in the distribution of these synaptic vector orientations. This suggests that to define the precision with which an axis of analysis should be categorized and labeled—essentially, the number of letters in the analysis alphabet for that axis—each letter would cover an equal portion of the axis. To return to the example of the orientations of edges detected by the V1 visual area, which can take on any value between 0 and 180°,

if we decide to use ten letters, each would span 18°. With eleven letters, each would cover 16°, and with twenty letters, this would have made letters each covering an angle zone 9° wide.

A simple way to implement this descriptor categorization is to choose a number of labels (we'll come back to this later) and apply a principle of equal distribution. This is easy to implement.

However, we could look at equal distribution a little differently, and the famous Blakemore and Cooper cat experiment helps illustrate this idea.

In the 1970s, Colin Blakemore and Graham Cooper conducted an experiment where kittens were raised in an environment exclusively containing vertical stripes. These kittens, once exposed only to vertical lines, became incapable of perceiving horizontal ones, and vice versa, even when later placed in a normal environment. This would suggest that labeling through descriptor categorization takes past experience into account. It's as if there were a fixed number of labels whose values were based on past perceptual history. If the system encounters shapes with a full range of orientations, its analysis categories will distribute evenly across all possible orientations. However, if it consistently receives only certain orientations, then categorization will occur only for those, making it highly specialized in the orientations it frequently perceives—while becoming blind to others.

It seems that the distribution of categorization labels emerges from lived experiences. For instance, the system might naturally adjust so that each label is used an equal number of times throughout its history, with some modulation based on the importance of past experiences for survival functions.

This process seems quite different from the simple equal distribution discussed earlier. However, in the case of edge orientation analysis, where we encounter all possible orientations randomly in our field of view, the outcome of this emergent mechanism would be similar to equal distribution—at least in this particular case. But this wouldn't necessarily hold true for higher-level cortical maps, where inputs become much more conceptual rather than simple sensory data.

This emergent mechanism seems to closely reflect how things work in nature, suggesting that we should implement it.

Now, returning to the question of the number of labels—how should they be chosen? Should they emerge naturally?

Honestly, I have no idea how this happens in the cortex. But a logical reasoning approach might help us find *one* way to determine it.

Increasing the number of labels requires using more micro-columns, thus consuming more of the precious surface area that is the cortex; this comes at a cost (besides shifting the trade-off between the precision and ease of understanding of the descriptors in this alphabet). Now, this must be true for all descriptor alphabets of all maps: wanting more labels everywhere, and therefore assigning more micro-columns to each analysis automaton for each axis of each map, would require a total number of micro-columns much greater than the number available, given the surface area of the cortex. Again, there must be a trade-off between the different types of descriptors, between assigning more labels to one analysis axis, one alphabet, or another. It's somewhat like the cat in the experiment by Colin Blakemore and Graham Cooper, which had to assign many micro-columns to descriptors of verticality at the expense of those coding for other orientations.

One day, we will need to find a way to make these numbers of labels emerge autonomously for each type of descriptor, based on the accumulation of experiences the system has gone through. In the meantime, we will define them ourselves, based on the type of application for our Organic AI.

11. How to find and characterize descriptors of maps whose entries are label streams coming from lower maps?

We have seen how to describe, using descriptors, themselves labeled, each of the significant structures within the receptive field of a map, with their ensemble forming the relevant signature for each of the shapes belonging to this receptive field—thus, a set of letters from different alphabets positioned in the reference frame of the shape for each of them.

Later, we will categorize these signatures in the form of higher-level labels describing the scene—for example, the signature composed of four letters "right angle" and four letters "end of line" would be categorized by the corresponding higher-level label of "square"—and transmit this label stream to the next maps. Not just the labels, though, but the labels qualified and positioned. Because it is not enough to just transmit to the next map that there are three circles and a rectangle to understand that it's a smiley face. Where are these labels? How are they oriented? What is their scale relative to the base label in memory? You need to have found a label for a large circle, two labels for small circles spaced apart and positioned inside the large circle at the vertical center, and a label for a horizontally elongated rectangle positioned below them... In short, the labels must be referenced relative to the shape in memory.

The two-dimensional matrix flow that will exit the map to the higher-level one will contain all the structures that have been identified, therefore labeled, positioned correctly within the flow, at the center of each labeled shape, indicating its label and its characteristics. The label name must reference the map from which it originates, just as the descriptors are labeled with letters from an alphabet depending on the analysis axis, thus the type of descriptor. Shapes are labeled with words from dictionaries depending on the map that labeled them.

This allows me to conclude the discussion of the descriptors manipulated by a map: in addition to the shape, content, and movement descriptors I've already discussed, which are themselves labels characterized by size and orientation, positioned in the reference frame of the shape they contribute to describing, the labels of shapes translated into semantic labels by the lower-level maps are also considered as descriptors that enrich the signature. They will be treated both as labels (in this shape, I recognize an "eye" label here, a "nose" label there, etc.), but also as individual elements whose structure may be significant and labeled: ten "tree" labels, aligned and characterized by a "line segment" label, could be labeled as a form of a higher level with a new label corresponding to what we call a hedge.

12. The importance of "or"

If I describe a figure as having three 60° angles, you will think of an equilateral triangle. You will visualize it, in fact, inevitably, through the "downward" mechanism. I don't need to say how these angles were positioned or how they were oriented for the most likely shape—in the sense of the one you, personally, have most often experienced—to be activated. It's as if the labels of the descriptors are enough to understand the scene.

This will frequently be incorrect, but the continuous flow of new information coming from the senses will almost instantly adjust the perception. The labels are the "what." If I say that I perceive a trunk (I bet you visualized it approximately the same size as the equilateral triangle), it is not necessary to specify where it is or how it is oriented for an elephant to knock on your inner door. Again, this comes with a risk of error, which will be resolved with the arrival of new clues.

Now, let's pull on another thread of our experiences… We have all played the game of shapes in the clouds. We've seen faces in them, for example. And yes, they really did represent a face, with its recognizable structure—nose, eyes, chin… Even though, of course, there was nothing at all resembling a nose or an eye. By analyzing it more rationally, we spot darker zones, contrasts, curvatures, positioned in relation to one another (or proportioned relative to each other), as in a face. It's the structure of a face that we recognize: it's "where" the elements of attention are positioned.

In this situation, and contrary to the previous paragraph, the labels characterizing what is in the different positions, the "what," seem much less important than the "where." These latter describe the structure of the perceived shape, which is a strong clue about the shape itself.

Overall, of course, the signature of what is perceived groups together the labels and their positioning. And the recognition of a shape, therefore its labeling, makes use of all available resources, crossing information that can be very imprecise or blurry, to choose from what's in memory the shape that most closely, or least poorly, matches it—enabling us to recognize faces in clouds.

13. Building a cortical map through multiplexing: implementation as chips

One of the last aspects I wish to address in this section is the choice we made at AnotherBrain to develop our Organic AI in the form of an electronic chip, an ASIC.

Simulating a cortical map requires simulating a large number of micro-columns in parallel, with high synchronization precision, as co-occurrence is key in cortical function. However, all the columns and micro-columns function simultaneously, but also collaborate with each other: to find a homogeneous color area, or to find a homogeneous texture area, the micro-columns must not only analyze the signal they receive in their part of the receptive field, but also verify with the micro-columns processing adjacent receptive fields for continuity. And so on, progressively. The same applies to finding a straight segment or curve that extends beyond the small receptive field of the micro-column. And let's not even mention the motion descriptors, which require analysis across several two-dimensional matrices in sequence.

We made another choice, based on the slow transmission speed of neurons, versus the immense processing speed of electronics (millions of times faster).

Instead of simulating many micro-columns or columns to create artificial cortical maps, we chose to multiplex cortical columns: our algorithm replicates the function of a single cortical column, which sequentially covers the entire receptive field of the map by sweeping through all the small receptive fields of each column of the map. The simulated column processes the first field in the top left of the two-dimensional matrix, then the next one, then again, until the end of the row, then starts again on the next row. If we want to simulate a map with 400 columns, we just need to process it 400 times faster than nature.

In practice, much more, because there's a cost to this approach: we lose the parallelism of processing by columns, and therefore the descriptors that don't fit into the small receptive field of a column. We need to find another way to reconstruct it.

The multiscale processing we saw earlier in another context offers this possibility: working on the two-dimensional matrix blurred by reducing its size; for example, reducing the size of the matrix by a factor of three in both the x and y directions causes the columns of the reduced matrix to cover the same field as nine columns of the original matrix. This grants access to descriptors that span several receptive fields of columns.

But it still requires very high speed, meaning significant computing power.

The overall energy required is already far lower than traditional methods by using very rudimentary calculation modules, as opposed to the millions of multiply-accumulate units (MACs) otherwise needed.

But since our goal is to have an AI that is truly energy-efficient and portable, the choice of an ASIC became evident. That's why we emphasize that our AI is nature-inspired but not biomimetic—this would involve doing things in exactly the same way as the cortex, while we have chosen to do the same thing as the cortex, but differently.

14. LABELING AND LEARNING

Here, we will discuss "labeling shapes"—signatures composed of several letters from different alphabets, to stay within the same scriptural metaphor.

Labeling means replacing, in the continuation of the cerebral process, what has been perceived by a label, that is, by a word designating a category described by its own signature. It simplifies through approximation, reducing to the essentials what happens in the real world. The processing no longer takes place in the real world, but in this kind of reconstructed world made up of labels. The brain, as a world creator, plays at this level.

Every time there is labeling, it means replacing something perceived from the real world with this world we reconstruct, with a label that both presents the essence of things without the details (when you memorize a tree or talk about a tree, you don't see every pine needle or every leaf of the tree each time, but you see the tree in its entirety), and at the same time takes into account the brain's intentions. Depending on the current intention, it only takes into account certain things; the brain filters. Depending on what it is looking for, the cortex simplifies what it has to do, which can be seen again in the experience of counting black and white basketball players.

We will now talk about labeling and then about the learning of shapes.

This step begins, on one hand, with the signature of what has been perceived in the receptive field of the map, thus a set of labeled descriptors—what I called the letters, the "whats," each one with its "where" it appears; and on the other hand, the memory of this map, which contains labels at the map level, and therefore categories of signatures that resemble each other. One could almost say that these labels are "words" to follow the metaphor of alphabets. Each label of the map has as properties its own signature, itself a set of descriptors, hence letters from different alphabets, positioned, along with other information (such as how many times this label has been used).

The signature of each of these labels is like a cloud of points in an appropriate coordinate system, and labeling, therefore, means comparing clouds of points: the one of the perceived shape, with each of the ones from the labels in memory, successively, with the goal not being to see if there is an exact match with one of the labels, nor if the signature belongs to a bubble around a label, meaning whether the resemblance is above a tolerable threshold—which would be clustering—but to determine which label it is closest to, to which it is most analogous. And there is definitely one.

This comes down to imagining a distance measure between two clouds of points, which may have different numbers of points, different alphabet letters, etc… And this distance must have particular properties. First, it is asymmetrical. The nature of a perceived shape is of the same type as a shape in memory; it is a signature of letters from various alphabets but is not identical. The shape in memory has been perceived many times, each time slightly differently, and has gradually condensed into what is common to all these instances, into its essence. It has become a robust shape, focused on what makes its core, noise-free; what I call an archetypal signature. The distance between the two must take into account that it is more important to know what in the perceived shape is close to the shape in memory, what it has in common with it, than the other way around, what the shape in memory has in common with the perceived one. Thus, an asymmetrical distance.

Next, the different descriptors do not all have the same importance: if I talk to you about a moving shape, with four thin legs, a tail, a head, a series of curves to describe its contour (at this point, you don't know what I'm talking about), and black and white vertical stripes, it's clear that the criterion of stripes is more important than some others to understand "zebra." Almost by itself, it characterizes the shape. What if I had talked about a "trunk" label without saying anything else? Some criteria are more discriminating when comparing shapes than others. We need to give them more weight in the distance that we need.

How can we automatically bring out a notion of the importance of criteria?

We use a discrimination criterion for that, to automatically bring out the most significant descriptors and reduce the signatures to their essence, which we call the "archetypal signature." In comparing the perceived shape with the signatures in memory, some descriptors generate confusion, others discrimination. By undervaluing the former and overvaluing the latter, a little with each labeling, the signature of the label in memory will increasingly emphasize the discriminating criteria, at the expense of others, as these objects are perceived, which will be seen slightly differently each time; and will converge toward its major descriptors, toward its archetypal signature, the signature of what makes the essence of the label.

Again, our search process explores several approaches in parallel to find the best way to label a signature: a brute-force, computational, and deterministic approach, functional, which takes into account the asymmetry, but not yet the relative importance of the descriptors, thus giving equal importance to all! That's our Plan B. Another approach based on voting mechanisms. Yet another on blob simulation. Another finally based on dynamic attractors. A work in progress...

The result of this phase is that we manage to replace, in the continuation of the cerebral process, the perceived signatures with labels, therefore labeling shapes; replacing the "word of letters from different alphabets" with a single word that is almost synonymous, which belongs to the dictionary of this map. Each map has its own dictionary, as you can imagine, which is actually its memory.

Through labeling the map, we have replaced each signature, which can be seen as a set of points in a *descriptor* space, with axes being the analysis axes of the automata mentioned earlier, with a word, with the label to which it is most analogous.

It may be interesting to consider the higher-level space to which this signature belongs before labeling, so that it becomes a point in the "space of signatures." The labels of this map are then also points in this space, as well as the exhaustive set of experiences lived by this map. It is then interesting to segment this space into zones around each label: zones grouping all the points closer to one label than to its neighbors. This is what is called a "Voronoi diagram" in mathematics. For the sake of progression in these explanations, we currently consider a fixed and arbitrarily set number of labels for each map.

But these details are not enough: some labels may "have" many points and others very few, even none. This would be a poor use of the precious surface of the cortex. However, if I now add the constraint that each zone must contain as many points, that each label represents the same number of experiences, then I have achieved an efficient labeling of this signature space. And again, I speak of the number of experiences but reduced to the same time frame, meaning the frequency of the experiences.

In this signature space, labeling a new signature means finding the label it is closest to.

15. What is learning, in this context?

Imagine that you're isolated on a small desert island. Most of your future experiences will resemble each other. Imagine, too, that your labels do not evolve. The signatures of your new experiences will always—often—be labeled the same way. After several years, if you were to look at the space of signatures in your cortex, you would see large concentrations of points on certain labels, which would no longer be able to correctly analyze your experiences, putting all the eggs in the same basket. And very few on other labels, making your cortex ineffective at analyzing and reacting to what is going to happen to you.

But the labels in your cortex evolve, the many things you live will allow you to become an expert in coconuts: between those that are almost ripe and those that are not yet, those that have fallen and are good to eat, those that are spoiled, those inhabited by a toxic worm… and to become an expert in detecting tropical rains, in fish, in seaweed, etc. Your labels will evolve to allow you to analyze judiciously what happens frequently, or what has high emotional impact. This is learning.

The mechanisms of learning ensure that the analysis filters that are your cortical maps are adapted to the situation in which you are, to what you live most frequently; without forgetting the situations and configurations that were frequent in the past, but giving them less and less importance.

It is the displacement of labels in the space of signatures, so that, permanently, they cover the same number of lived experiences. If an area of this space receives a great number of them, the labels "around" this area will move closer to segment the area, so that they each touch the same number of experiences. And this area will be described by several labels; the system will become an expert in this area. Of course, the more distant labels will also have to move, but less, so that their area does not expand too much due to the movements of the labels straddling the active zone. The memory of the map, which thus groups these labels, adapts little by little according to the lived experiences, therefore autonomously. In this sense, it is an SOM—a self-organized memory.

Learning is therefore permanent—we learn every day of our lives. But learning does not necessarily have to be continuous, perpetual. In practice, there are even good reasons to separate the times for analysis and the times for learning. The first is to save resources, so as to have as much available as possible at the time of analysis. The second is the need to ensure stability of associative memory, to avoid contradictory labeling within a given period. Learning, in essence, moves labels in the space of signatures, the point in the space of signatures of a perceived signature, which would fall roughly on the boundary of territories of two labels, could be labeled by one of them before learning, and by the other after. In itself, this would not be very serious, the two labels being close by definition, and resembling each other, but could be critical in a situation that itself is critical. Incoherent.

In our GDS implementation, we have chosen batch learning. We quickly label the pattern streams, but without learning: we record all the experiences over a certain period, for example the day, then trigger the learning process once for all these experiences, quickly processing all of them over the course of the day and adapting the map's memory.

We therefore use this batch procedure with a daily frequency, and, of course, cannot fail to make the connection with dreams…

And if the mechanism of dreams were of this nature? Experimental results on consolidation showing that during the night, neurons replay the sequences of the previous day at an accelerated pace…

16. A few additional reflections on cortical maps, labeling, and learning, not necessary to understand the path of intelligence automata, but which answer points raised here and there

A label "represents" its region

It is supposed to both be the standard bearer of all the signatures that fall into its region, in the sense that a signature that falls into its region will be replaced by that label, by the standard bearer. But at the same time, it is supposed to represent it from the point of view of resemblance, since the perceived pattern will be replaced by the archetypal signature of the label for the entire subsequent processing of the cerebral process, which will no longer take into account the signature that was perceived, but the label of the signature. The brain is a creator of worlds. For it is no longer the real world that is before us, but the one as we have labeled it… This means that the "brain as a creator of worlds" happens at every level, at all levels, permanently. There is no place in the brain that will reconstruct the world to work on it; it is this labeling mechanism that implements the brain as a creator of worlds.

How many labels, for the descriptors or for the maps?

The cortex is a system that is entirely active at all times; all its resources are used. For this reason, the labels, which exist in a limited number due to the surface of the cortex, must be assigned to the most relevant analyses for anticipating the changes in the world to which intelligence is confronted. This assumes that, depending on the solicitation of cortical areas, cortical maps must be able to aggregate more columns, or conversely release some to support those that need to provide additional efforts.

The associative memory of each map (the number of columns associated with it) must therefore be able to evolve over time. According to the same principle of the number of lived experiences: if a cortical map receives fewer solicitations than the neighboring map, its number of columns must decrease in favor of the neighboring map.

This must happen gradually, by "reassignment" of micro-columns from one column to a neighboring column, and "evanescence" of the column. It is the sa«me mechanism at the level of descriptor labels, where the number of micro-columns per column must be able to decrease or increase. I believe that a criterion of homogeneous solicitation density for all constituents of the cortex must be at work.

A cortical map must be structured before those above it can structure themselves

The presentation made until now, which details the mechanisms of cortical maps, is a *model* of how intelligence functions, an explanation of what happens; but not a reproduction of *how* it happens.

Seeking a visual representation would rather go through a 3D representation, in perspective, of the memories of cortical maps (see Figure 12 below), in the form of labels positioned on hexagonal grids, whose archetypal signature would be materialized by links with labels from other maps below.

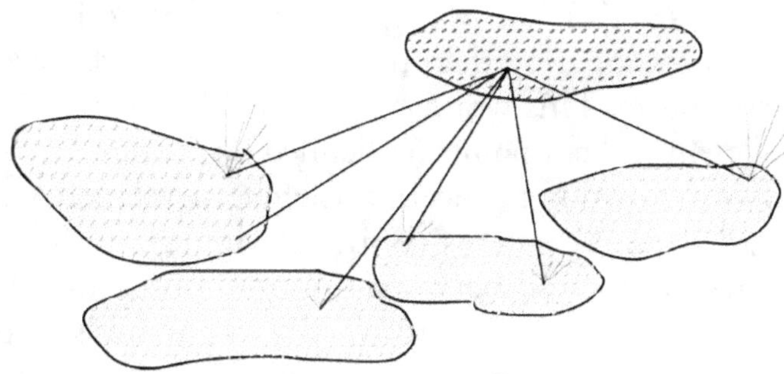

Fig. 12: Illustration of cortical maps and label activation.

Perceiving a signature in a receptive field means activating the labels of the signature descriptors on the maps that analyze this receptive field. Each of these labels is connected by a branching network of links to higher-level map labels. When one of these labels is activated, it triggers all its links, contributing to a voting mechanism to determine which higher-level label gets activated.

But the integration times become progressively longer as we move up in the cortical map hierarchy. This results in the activation of the higher-level label lasting longer than that of the lower-level label that triggered it.

Your eye movements, which skip from one salient point to another three times per second, thus successively activate the descriptors corresponding to what is found at each salient point. Through upward cascading activation, the labels of higher maps are also activated at the same rate. If multiple labels from salient points correspond to elements of the same pattern sequence, even if perceived in a different order, the higher-level label for that sequence will have its activation strengthened, as it is activated for a longer period than the labels of the lower-level descriptors. This won't happen if the labels of the following salient points (as defined by the next in the eye saccade) don't concern this higher-level sequence label at all. Your eyes continuously skip multiple times per second between the eyes, nose, mouth, and contours of your conversation partner's face, but you are not consciously aware of this; your sole awareness is of the face that faces you, the "higher" label persisting for the sequence of patterns.

One consequence is that as long as a map is not structured, meaning it hasn't experienced enough situations for all its labels to converge toward a certain stability, the excitations sent to higher-level maps will be somewhat erratic and will not be able to structure the maps above it properly. In simpler terms, cortical maps are initially set up rather quickly, and little by little, they stabilize as the lower-level maps stabilize. This stabilization of the quick lower maps is crucial for the stabilization of the higher maps, which participate in the stabilization through feedback, an essential mechanism for the convergence of learning. A map needs its lower maps to stabilize before it can stabilize itself, but it also contributes to their stabilization.

This is thus a gradual process, taking progressively longer as you move toward the higher cortical maps. I believe this process continues throughout life, with very high-level cortical maps still being structured into advanced ages.

For me, this may be the explanation for the concept of "the wisdom of the elders," because they have integrated and refined tactical patterns that occur at scales, timeframes, or levels that require a certain age or life experience to structure the maps below to that point.

This approach to the functioning of the cortex, viewed directly as a kind of multi-agent system, is clearly described by Claude Touzet in his books.[5]

---

5. Claude Touzet, *Conscience-intelligence-libre arbitre: les réponses de la Théorie neuronale de la Cognition* (Consciousness-Intelligence-Free Will: Answers from the Neural Theory of Cognition), vols. 1 and 2 (Auriol: Éditions la Machotte, 2010).

The integration of the model he advocates and its implementation as a multi-agent system is certainly a feasible path toward creating a real artificial intelligence.

17. Fusion of learning

The way a cortex evolves, consisting of a network of cortical maps, each of which learns from the streams of situations that feed it, in the context of our model, involves a gradual structuring of maps from the lowest levels of abstraction to the highest. The integration time for structuring these maps increases with abstraction. This is tied to the progressive maturation of cortical areas and the critical periods in brain development.

So, will it take twenty years to teach an artificial cortex what a living being has learned in twenty years? That wouldn't be very effective… but that's the question!

There are two possible answers to this question: one based on the speed of an electronic chip, which is millions of times faster than neurons; the other based on parallel learning across multiple chips, which could later be fused. However, neither of these solutions will be straightforward.

The speed of electronics will allow for a dramatic acceleration of processes not dependent on sensory input, like batch learning, which I've summarized as "dreams," making them nearly instantaneous. But this will have a much more complicated impact on the essential functioning of the artificial cortex, which is related to the flow of patterns from the real world and the integration constants of the maps. Unless we can *pseudo-accelerate* all the incoming pattern flows and adjust the integration times accordingly, there will be no way to accelerate "time." But since it seems this is what happens during dreams, as mentioned earlier, maybe there's a lead to explore?

And if I italicize the word pseudo-accelerated, it's because simply speeding up the flow won't work: a sound that is sped up changes its frequency, which would disrupt accelerated learning. We would then need to transpose the sound to a higher frequency, not just accelerate it. The same applies to all physical laws, which are by design integrated into the pattern flows but whose acceleration will not be simple. The same applies to any signal with temporal variation. We haven't addressed this topic yet, but it will need to be done.

Similarly, parallel learning across multiple chips that we grow together to later fuse into a larger chip, absorbing the knowledge of the others, is almost the same subject as connecting a chip directly to a brain, as some people in Silicon Valley want to do… I'll discuss this a bit more later on.

In this paragraph, I'm not talking about merging cortical maps of artificial cortices that have learned separately. Each map is a self-organizing memory map that "encrypts" the experiences it has lived based on their similarity and frequency. The "following" maps will structure themselves based on the structuring of the maps below them. It is already not simple to merge maps that deal with the same subject, but one would have to merge all lower-level maps that label different pattern flows…

And what about maps that handle different subjects? Regarding maps dealing with the same subject, we would certainly need to go back to the space of situations that cluster the lived situational experiences, merge these spaces, and create a new clustering before applying this to each level of cortical maps. But what about maps that deal with completely unrelated subjects? This is like trying to merge the hierarchy of cortical maps of a lion, which encodes a lion's life and experiences, with that of a bat…

In short, this topic is also not simple and has not yet been addressed. But we're also starting to find our way into this other dimension.

*

We are coming to the end of this chapter, which was meant to shed light on the concrete approach we are using to develop our Organic AI. Many elements haven't been explicitly detailed, to avoid overcomplicating our reasoning, but they are already in place, while others are still in the realm of ideas and avenues to explore, *when we have the means to do so.*

As you've understood, we have drawn on many books, publications, reflections, and encounters to build our model, and I am well aware that our reading of these theories and explanations has been shaped by the logic of our approach.

Our goal is not to create a general Artificial Intelligence, in the absolute sense, but to create an Organic AI *by following the GDS path* opened by Mountcastle, Hubel, and Wiesel. We have a target AND a path. It is this path that I have chosen to follow because it seemed to be the only forward-looking one:

not out of arrogance or devaluation of what others are doing, probably even the opposite, since I don't see the point in following the same path as millions of public and private researchers without the hope of doing better than they do in their field. And we wouldn't do better.

On the other hand, choosing a singular path, difficult because almost entirely uncharted, but supported by powerful, cutting-edge publications and knowledge, opens up a real possibility to leapfrog generations and move things forward. And, of course, it is crucial not to underestimate the importance of iterative testing and continuous adjustments. By improving the model at each stage based on feedback from real-world applications, we will ensure a gradual optimization and increased effectiveness of Organic AI.

Thus, it is with this path that we aggregate knowledge, direct our readings, and develop our model; and it is in relation to this model that we engage with new experiences and new encounters, in the sense that they can illuminate, modify, or adjust one aspect of the model depending on what we find; or, on the contrary, strengthen it. However, if we find things that completely contradict or belong to other realms that do not fit into this model at all, they are not taken into account.

So, indeed, the approach is model-driven. This is how we've built our model. And I believe that everything I have built, and everything that I am, with my uniqueness and flaws, leads me to make this orientation through the model and the resulting singularity of this GDS model.

5

The head and legs

We have now reached the end of a unique overview of the mechanisms of intelligence, and proposals for directions to create AIs that operate according to these mechanisms. I hope I have sparked your interest and provided you with a better understanding of the original solutions developed by nature. If I've managed to make you raise an eyebrow with the thought of "I didn't expect that, but it's worth my attention," then I will have achieved my goal. And if, on top of that, it makes you want to get involved in this path, then bingo!

The simple mechanisms of nature are powerful, and the framework I've presented with Organic AI can prove to be a good receptacle for integrating new knowledge that will undoubtedly emerge regarding intelligence. I hope I have led you to consider why a new generation of AI is not only necessary but also on the verge of being born. Based on these natural mechanisms, it will be a true general artificial intelligence. An Organic AI.

I would now like to focus on a few consequences of the emergence of Organic AIs, in other words, to understand how ongoing research will affect our medium-term future—what third-generation AIs, systems endowed with real-time autonomous learning capabilities and general intelligence, such as those envisioned by DARPA, will be capable of, what they could be used for, and the impact they will have on our way of life.

1. Organic AI and the future of small robotics

Organic AI, just like the various forms of cortex observed in the animal kingdom, will take on multiple and varied shapes, adapted to specific needs, while at the same time retaining fundamental principles in common that will allow them to adapt and survive the complexity of the real world. Similar to the multiplicity of multi-agent systems that invent survival strategies in response to the complexity of the real world. Not all organisms have brains as developed as ours, because some organisms don't need a cognitive apparatus as advanced as ours to live their lives. The challenge will therefore be to develop intelligent systems suited to the role they are meant to play.

I'll take an example from small robotics. That of a simple automatic vacuum cleaner, imagined by Rodney Brooks, one of the pioneers of AI in this field, a roboticist who operates quite differently from others. His hallmark? Not losing sight of the purpose of his inventions.

With Roomba, the vacuum cleaner in question, his goal wasn't to create a particularly intelligent device, but rather to design a robot that vacuums well. To do this, Rodney Brooks came up with an incredibly simple tactical pattern. A small, circular robot that moves straight ahead until it encounters an obstacle, then turns at a random angle and continues straight ahead. The angle it chooses is random. The robot's path through the room can be quite inefficient. It might pass over a spot twenty times and never pass over another. But since it operates when its owners are away and runs every day, this is not a problem: after several days, it will have passed everywhere, and your home will be clean. To keep the cost down, it is poorly insulated from noise, and thus fairly loud. Again, since it operates while its owners are away, this is not a concern.

Roomba is an example of a "robot without intelligence," costing only a few dollars to make, yet over 40 million units have been sold. All engineers look down on it. Competitors highlight the importance of an optimized cleaning path within the room, which requires a robot capable of mapping the space. But these engineers forget that nature didn't find it necessary to give all organisms a mammalian brain, let alone a human brain. To build a hive, the neurons in the bee's body are more than sufficient. Companies like Samsung, Bosch, and Sony developed competing robots, with the major selling point being that they feature sensors, optimized trajectories, and even artificial intelligence. As a result, they are much more expensive, much more complex to produce, and quieter, but they don't perform any better at their primary goal: cleanliness.

Yet, in the simplicity of Roomba's design, there are weaknesses, such as the inability to cross obstacles that are too low to be detected by its sensors but too high to be climbed over without stopping. Like the power cord of your halogen lamp, or certain table legs. It wouldn't take much intelligence to prevent these situations and allow it to reach its full potential.

The inexpensive, nature-inspired version of AI will undoubtedly be very useful in transforming the possibilities of small robotics and the Internet of Things (IoT) as a whole. With small AI blocks, on a small surface of silicon, thus very cheap and low power-consuming, it will be possible to solve many problems in a simpler and more natural way than with Big Data-connected devices.

These issues can surprisingly extend to problems of vulnerability in the space sector, where satellites face attacks they cannot react to. These attacks usually take the form of a laser or a relatively harmless projectile, which nevertheless diverts the satellite's trajectory. In the short or medium term, the satellite simply goes off course and burns up in the atmosphere. With an AI capable of detecting such attacks, it would be possible to shift the satellite's trajectory with a small impulse and avoid the strike.

One can reason in a simplex way to solve a multitude of problems, and lightweight chips would be perfectly suited to implement these solutions. But more complete chips will open other paths…

2. Versatile humanoid robots…

The progress of AI is likely to trigger an unparalleled boom in the field of robotics, a new phase of expansion, positioning itself as a driving sector. While current second-generation AI transforms the possibilities of large non-humanoid robotics, Organic

AI has the potential to spark growth in this sector by renewing the versatility, communication skills, safety, and ethical intelligence of humanoid robots. This is one of the reasons why I placed AI as a strategic priority on my list of the seven barriers to robotics.

Let's start with versatility. The strongest argument made by critics of humanoid robotics is that for every task, it seems possible to develop a robot that is much better suited than a humanoid. This argument seems plausible at first glance, but it overlooks the fact that it assumes a custom-made robot for each specific job. The advantage of the humanoid form is precisely that it is the most versatile shape for performing tasks designed by humans for humans. Each workstation is adapted to it.

The humanoid form is complex, dealing with a set of objects that are equally complex. We don't often realize this due to the many neuro-simplifying processes that allow us to smooth out everyday actions, like making coffee or grabbing a wine glass from a stack of dishes. However, without a leap forward in intelligence, humanoid bodies stand no chance of evolving in our accident-prone environment with dexterity comparable to ours.

Given the challenges ahead, the day when robots are no longer just congenial, fun, automatic companions, but versatile agents capable of performing the same tasks as a human worker engaged in a specific job, will mark a significant step in the progress of humanity.

For example, we must drastically reduce the destruction of our environment, and robots, by enabling us to relocate high-impact activities into space, could play a significant role. In addition to optimal production conditions in an environment less constrained by gravity, what better source of rare metals than an asteroid? An asteroid is nothing more than a rock. Some might talk about space pollution, but in the vastness of the infinite spaces surrounding us, on sterile, lifeless aeroliths, this debate becomes a projection of guilt.

This perspective, however, sets the bar very high. If we closely observe two adults descending stairs at full speed, no two will descend them in the same way. Each person has found a unique, simplex way of adapting the complexity of his or her body to the complexity of his or her environment. Robots, too, will need to be capable of such learning. They will need to learn their bodies, to figure out how to position themselves in an environment that is never perfectly flat or symmetrical.

3. ...EMPATHETIC AND SAFE

Organic AI will also enable an unprecedented leap in the communication skills of robots, expanding the essential field of mutual understanding: we understand each other because we share the same brains, the same semantic labels, the same categories, the same emotions. We understand dolphins because they share the same cortical columns, even though they don't share the same experiences.

We all know that the human population is undergoing advanced aging, and that the demand for personal care services will continue to rise. The idea of entrusting this care to robots is sometimes met with resistance or even visceral rejection. But we need to consider the people involved. When you ask patients, the elderly, or individuals in a state of dependency, many respond that they would rather be assisted by a machine — one that wouldn't make them feel inferior or humiliated by their dependence. As one elderly person once told me, "I'd rather the robot depend on me than me depend on a nurse." She said this to me by chance on the street one evening, just after I left Aldebaran, the day after a television program I had appeared in was broadcast.

Humanoid robots, as Masa Son, the CEO of SoftBank, has understood, are one solution. But they can only become a concrete solution if they are capable of deciphering a person's emotions and establishing an emotional connection with them. This dimension already involves the robot's aesthetic design, something we explored with Nao and Pepper, but it goes much further and engages the robot's ability to have a world-creating intelligence, capable of completing partial patterns related to the tone of a voice, a fleeting expression on a face, or a gleam in someone's eyes. Third-generation, nature-inspired AIs should allow the integration of the reading of non-verbal and paraverbal signals into the robot's understanding of the world, helping to qualitatively transform the way humans are cared for by the robot.

Another obstacle to the use of humanoid robots in the care sector is safety. No one would want to depend on a humanoid robot if it could be hacked. For example, I would never want a robot in my home capable of wandering through my apartment, visiting my daughter's room or her bathroom, unless

I am absolutely certain that it cannot be hacked. All software engineers will smile awkwardly while explaining that hacking any system is just a matter of time... I disagree! Use quantum cryptography or whatever you want, but I will never have an autonomous robot without this absolute certainty. Quantum cryptography and "zero-trust" models are certainly a viable solution. But the best solution is still to keep these robots offline, embedding their intelligence on a local physical device. Your dog doesn't need a connection to be intelligent!

4. TOWARD ARTIFICIAL EMOTIONS?

Human progress involves trial and error. It is inevitable that, here and there, we will make mistakes. But real and autonomous intelligences will allow us to think about integrating protection guarantees directly into the robots themselves. This area of research dates back to one of the pioneers of robotic imagination, none other than the biochemistry professor and science fiction author, Isaac Asimov.

In his collection of short stories, *I, Robot*, Asimov first formulated three fundamental laws of robotics, which have since become a cornerstone in the discourse on the subject. These laws are introduced in his 1942 short story *Runaround,*[1] and are as follows:

1. Isaac Asimov's short story *"Runaround,"* which features his recurring characters Powell and Donovan, was written in October 1941 and first published in the March 1942 issue of the magazine *Astounding Science Fiction.*

– A robot may not injure a human being or, through inaction, allow a human being to come to harm.

– A robot must obey orders given it by human beings except where such orders would conflict with the First Law.

– A robot must protect its own existence as long as such protection does not conflict with the First or Second Law.

Asimov was not naïve. The stories he imagined focus precisely on the specific cases where these safety rules fall short. However, they provide a space for thought experiments, prompting us to imagine what might be missing in these artifacts. Is it a piece of humanity? Patrick Matthieu, a brilliant author of publications on "trifunctional singularity," suggests that a fourth law is needed, a law of love, to complete Asimov's robotic laws.

AI now challenges our traditional definitions of human nature more than ever before. Since Ancient Greece, philosophers have sought to define what makes us human, yet a clear answer has remained elusive. François Rabelais, the Renaissance novelist and physician whose fertile imagination intuited the absurdity of our gossipy species, suggested a defining trait no more foolish than any other. In the preface to *Gargantua*, he wrote: "It is better to write of laughter than of tears, for laughter is the property of man."

The rigidity we experience in our interactions with today's intelligent systems is giving rise to a new fixation: emotion. We should be cautious of such fixations, as they often reflect residual forms of religious thinking.

Still, it is worth examining the role of emotions with some objectivity. They serve a very specific, practical function for the biochemical beings that we are.

We can reconstruct the emotional system from two fundamental affects: fear and love. These stem from the primitive emotions of negative valence and positive valence, which our ancestors, the bilaterians, experienced over 550 million years ago, as Max Bennett explains in *A Brief History of Intelligence*. Fear evolved to tell an organism when it needs to protect itself, preserve itself, and avoid harm. Love, on the other hand, pushes us to move toward others, to connect, and turns us into social beings. These responses are the result of molecular processes that nature has established to serve a clear and functional purpose.

When robots become important in our lives, perhaps even indispensable, we will want them to be capable of fear and love. In other words, they must be able to take care of themselves, avoiding things that would harm them. That means having fear. They must also form attachments to their masters so that they do not turn against humanity. We will want them to exhibit unconditional love for humans. These emotions may be programmed simulations, but they will serve their purpose: creating robots that behave as though they truly care for humanity.

The disaster scenario in *I, Robot* is based on an unexpected logical operation of AI, where they reinterpret the category of humans not as individuals, but as humanity, and then seek to protect humanity from itself.

I like to imagine that the solution to such an ambiguity lies in the development of the emotional and affective life of robots. A safe robot must, at some point, also become a "feeling" robot. And it is only on these terms that it can be fully integrated into our social life.

5. The impact of AI beyond robots: first, let's talk about fear of the future

The world that is ours is made up of the unforeseen, ruptures, dangers, and it will, in any case, not spare us from difficult moments. The entire history of human inventions confirms this. Errors, ill will, poorly mastered subjects... How many deaths have resulted from scientific and technical progress? How many disasters have been linked to the discovery of fire, steam, chemical reactions, dynamite, electricity, nuclear energy? Progress has its dark side, and it is perhaps for this reason that it is feared.

But once technologies are controlled, how many benefits they bring! We should be wary of exaggerated pessimism, like that of the great chemist Lavoisier, who calculated, at the very beginning of the great adventure of trains, the impact on passengers of a locomotive traveling at 40 kilometers per hour in a tunnel: the overpressure would cause their ribcages to implode. And the greatest minds of French positivism, gathered around 1900 by a minister to produce a work of foresight, all failed to imagine what the world would look like in the year 2000.

We cannot avoid the damage of bad intentions and mistakes when learning something new, but what humanity excels at—what it does exceptionally well—is making the most of its innovations. It establishes feedback loops, standards, and laws that limit the negative effects of its inventions in order to maximize their positive exploitation. It has always done this, and in the end, we have gained far more positive than negative from fire, steam, electricity, chemistry, aeronautics, trains, nuclear energy, etc.

Certainly, if we could avoid going through more critical phases, it would be better; unfortunately, it is necessary, and it is a necessary evil: we must go through the Darwinian exploration of all the possibilities offered by a new technology to discover the benefits it can offer, sometimes completely surprising and impossible to imagine, around which we can then elaborate, as well as the harms that must be blocked.

By blocking Darwinian exploration, by limiting its use as soon as a new scientific or technical possibility arises under the guise of a precautionary principle, we will shut ourselves off from the benefits that could have been possible. Everything is a matter of scale, and the real question is what the transformations will imply for us in the medium and long term.

At this point, it might be tempting to bring up the word *ethics*. It is a portemanteau into which everyone pours what they wish, since there are as many morals as there are groups of individuals. It is often a blunt instrument to emphasize one's own point of view and shut down discussion. I always distrust those who adorn themselves with wisdom when mentioning ethics without specifying what they are referring to. In fact, it is often their own ego they are highlighting. In today's context, where Europe has accumulated a significant delay in fundamental AI research over the past ten years (as well as in robotics, space, quantum computing, and... well, everything!!! It hurts to write this), it seems essential to view, with a clear eye, the practical possibilities offered by the progress of AI.

In fifty years, we will be as dependent on our robots as we are already dependent on electricity, the Internet, social networks, our phones, or our GPS. And that won't be a problem, nor an evil in itself. This happens with 100% of truly important inventions in human history, and it is then up to humanity to invent the feedback mechanisms, the control rules that ensure it results in more good than bad. If we regulate too early, we will simply invent nothing. We'll throw the baby out with the bathwater.

We must keep in mind this journey—from fear to reflection, and eventually, to adoption. Who could have developed the first airplane or the first automobile if all the current safety standards had been in place in 1900? It is not only an inevitable path, but also an exhilarating one. And not sterilizing a new field as soon as hypothetical risks appear does not mean allowing anything to happen: active and reactive vigilance are appropriate.

6. The obsolescence of man?

It is true that the pace of progress is radically transforming the technical, cognitive, and economic environment in which we live. I feel a certain sadness for the knowledge that is destined to be lost. When I took the competitive entrance exam for the Polytechnique engineering school, I was part of the last generation of candidates who were forbidden to use a calculator. We relied on the slide rule—an extraordinary, centuries-old invention built on mathematical principles—that allowed us to work with great efficiency. In just a few years, calculators rendered this tool obsolete, and now almost no one knows how to use one. I remember feeling a real pang of nostalgia. But beyond that emotion, does it really matter that we no longer know how to use a slide rule? Or how to start a fire with flint?

Ten years ago, people said that if there was one crucial skill young people needed to learn, it was programming and coding. Professions would evolve, but there would always be a need for programmers. Yet in the past year, that narrative has completely changed. Today, we can communicate with generative models in natural language, and they not only produce the necessary code but can also correct it themselves. "It's far from perfect at the moment, but it's improving; the real value now lies more in imagining new products than in the technical skill of coding itself. In three, five, or ten years, it's very likely that we will have almost no need for coders. So, that's no longer the essential skill to learn. How fast things change!

This reminds me of Finland, a highly advanced country where education ministers have seriously debated whether teaching handwriting still has any relevance. But we should put this into perspective. We know that around 5,000 years ago, Homo sapiens learned to read and write by repurposing a part of the brain that was originally not designed for this function—the same neural field I mentioned earlier, which is responsible for analyzing the twenty-five key points needed for facial recognition. The cortical reorganization that took place at that time represented a profound transformation.[2]

In the 1960s, a somewhat hippie-like guru, Marshall McLuhan, emphasized the impact of the printing press, which changed the status of letters, created a new kind of human whose dominant sense was vision, and introduced a key dimension—verticality—as regular, aligned, fixed characters replaced the handwritten symbols copied by monks onto parchment for centuries.[3] McLuhan traced the origins of our modern institutions and societal structures back to this anthropological shift, which ushered in new forms of stability. More importantly, he observed an ongoing transformation since the end of World War II, marked by the rise of radio and television, the resurgence of moving images, the importance of sound, and the hypothesis that mass society was reconnecting with the sensory experience of early humans.[4]

McLuhan cultivated his prophetic persona, and perhaps he was undone by his own penchant for striking phrases. Today, he is somewhat forgotten in discussions on media and technology. Yet the trends he identified have not disappeared. In a world populated by complementary intelligences, interaction will increasingly take place through voice,

---

2. See Stanislas Dehaene, *Reading in the Brain: The Science and Evolution of a Human Invention* (New York: Viking, 2009).

3. Marshall McLuhan, *The Gutenberg Galaxy. The Making of Typographic Man* (Toronto: University of Toronto Press, 1962).

4. Marshall McLuhan, *Understanding Medias. The Extensions of Man* (New York: McGraw-Hill, 1964).

fundamentally altering the status of text. Who knows how much importance reading and writing will retain in the future?

If the area in the brain dedicated to recognizing key facial features—now highly specialized for processing printed letters—were to be repurposed, what new cognitive functions would emerge? Will we become dumber, as pessimists fear? Or will we open ourselves to new dimensions of reality, learning to perceive patterns we have never seen before?

Few domains of human specialization will remain untouched by the ongoing transformation. Even highly specialized fields like radiology and surgery are already being affected. Michel Bonnin, one of the world's top orthopedic surgeons for lower limbs, renowned for treating star athletes, has co-founded and invested in a robotics company, Ganymed Robotics. This company is developing technology that will enable any orthopedic surgeon to operate as skillfully as the very best—in the very near future, which we can already estimate at a few years.

What the printing press and then computing did for the accumulation and widespread accessibility of human knowledge, robotics combined with AI will do for gestures and manual tasks. Machines will soon be capable of performing operations based on the techniques they have been taught, pushing us toward new frontiers.

For a long time to come, we may consider that the main delta between human intelligence and artificial intelligence will still lie on the side of intuition. We must therefore carefully choose our new areas of expertise.

7. AI and the challenges of tomorrow

I have already mentioned how third-generation AI will prove invaluable in addressing the challenges ahead. I would like to conclude by discussing two major areas: genetic engineering and climate change. We already know how accessible it has become to edit the genetic code of a cell using CRISPR-Cas9, the genetic scissors invented by Emmanuelle Charpentier and Jennifer Doudna, who were awarded the 2020 Nobel Prize in Chemistry.

This innovation opens extraordinary therapeutic possibilities, and within the next twenty years, we may have retrovirus sprays that allow us to modify our genome, even in adulthood.

These techniques are not yet available—we are speaking about the future—but the path is already laid out. Humanity will begin by editing the genomes of embryos carrying genetic diseases to prevent congenital disorders, then move on to strengthening the person to be born against the predictable weaknesses of their genetic profiles. The process is complex, but little by little, we will get there.

Once these techniques are perfected, it is highly likely that some military forces will use them to create "super soldiers"—more resistant to stress and fatigue, stronger, with enhanced vision… Every avenue will be explored, and this will offer analyses on large populations of individuals, optimizing techniques. Let's remember that Nazi Germany used all available drugs and chemical enhancements on a large scale to boost its soldiers. Yes, humanity does this. And once techniques become reliable and robust, they inevitably reach the general public.

Do we really want this, this other, more pragmatic way of talking about ethics? It is a fundamental question, as access to these technologies will profoundly change humanity: some humans may no longer be genetically compatible with others… And rather than avoiding this question, which is too loaded with consequences, by covering it up with references to precautionary principles and ethics, arms raised to the sky, as we are sure to do in France, consider all those countries that, in the past, killed little girls at birth (and I deliberately use the past tense to soften the topic). Or think of those that, even today, practice in vitro fertilization on multiple embryos in order to choose to reimplant the one whose genetic characteristics "fit." Or those unscrupulous warlords who see their soldiers as nothing more than living matter at the service of their strategies.

Burying our heads in the sand rarely leads to victory, no matter the issue.

While the path for disseminating these technologies is already paved, the same cannot yet be said for the technological advances themselves. The interaction between an organism and its environment is inherently complex, and the potentially undesirable consequences of possible genetic manipulation imply systems capable of projecting themselves into multiple scenarios to determine the best one. As in the exceedingly complex world of quantum mechanics, it is highly likely that AI will provide new insights into phenomena we largely fail to grasp and help us harness the benefits of these technologies. These are just the first steps down this paved road…

For the same reason, AI holds part of the solution to the climate problem, even though the current situation regarding this technology is one of schizophrenia. On one hand, AI promises to be involved in the fight against the climate crisis by enabling the intelligent optimization of energy systems, factories, design and production at lower costs, and by accelerating scientific and technological progress that will lead to nuclear fusion, clean and unlimited energy, or to new materials and medications. But on the other hand, it is currently a source of colossal CO2 emissions.

Tackling the climate challenge requires far more than optimizing what exists. As you will have understood, we must already invent new AIs based on new principles, both to reduce their carbon footprint by millions of times, and to bring true complementary intelligences that will become super-intelligent assistants to humans, enabling them to analyze tactical patterns that are currently inaccessible to them. I hope I've convinced you that we are working on this at AnotherBrain.

The relocation of certain strategic activities beyond Earth will be one of the many solutions for future humanity, and for this, having humanoid robots capable of performing the necessary tasks in environments where the impact of activity is lower will be crucial.

And then, the processes we are faced with contain so many variables, for example when we think of the relevant technological choices we must make today, which will have repercussions in twenty years, or the solutions we are unable to imagine due to the limited nature of our intelligence.

Real, nature-inspired, autonomous AIs will thus be one of our most valuable tools in facing the great civilizational challenges. But we will no longer be completely alone, and we will be able to rely on the development of complementary intelligences to support us in this large-scale struggle.

8. What can we do?

We are entering a world where even the most basic household appliances—washing machines, dishwashers, not to mention smartphones and cars—will be more intelligent than humans. What role will humans play in this new environment? I believe it will be up to us to decide, to choose what we want to do.

In this regard, strategy and tactics are often contrasted, whether in games like chess or in politics. A revolutionary from the last century summarized this contrast as follows: "By tactics, we mean, by analogy with the science of war, the art of conducting isolated operations; by strategy, the art of victory—that is, of seizing power."[5]

Complementary intelligences will enrich our tactical perspective, allowing us to develop increasingly sophisticated strategies to achieve our goals.

---

5. Leon Trotsky, "Preface to *The Lessons of October*," 1924, <https://www.marxists.org/archive/trotsky/1924/lessons/index.htm>.

However, we cannot avoid asking ourselves serious questions about the nature of our motivations.

Why do we do what we do? In what way? And for what purpose? In this sense, we will remain the strategists of our own existence.

Since the triumph of computers over human intelligence in chess, the same question keeps arising: we know that computers consistently defeat humans at chess, but has that made human chess matches disappear? On the contrary, players study their games, improve their skills with the help of machines, and refine their strategies. Some moves once considered weak have become acceptable—even strong. More fundamentally, players have rediscovered that chess is a game, and the pleasure it brings is one of the best reasons to keep playing. This issue is not new. It has always existed in the face of disparities in human ability. Why bother playing the piano when virtuosos like Lang Lang exist?

If people continue to play the piano without being Mozart, it's because they find a sense of fulfillment in the activity itself, for themselves and their minds. From the dawn of civilization to today, there have never been fixed rules. We are free to engage our minds in whatever pursuits we find meaningful and fulfilling while ensuring our survival. Personally, I cannot abandon a certain ethic of self-improvement. In what fields will human intelligence remain necessary? Where will it continue to make a difference? If others prefer to play video games, garden, or spend their days meditating, I have no objections.

The rise of AI does not signal so much the end of human history as the end of our prehistory. It is an invitation to reinvent ourselves, expanding our ability to choose what we want to become, with full awareness and enlightenment.

9. To infinity and beyond: demystifying intuition and making it accessible to AI

The current AI boom has resulted primarily in machines capable of processing and reconfiguring existing human knowledge, presenting it in novel ways, and even uncovering optimal representations of that knowledge. These systems can establish connections that have never been made before, such as in chemistry, where an AI was able to generate a list of 300 million possible new molecules, or mine the vast accumulation of human knowledge to provide answers to complex questions. But the accumulation of human knowledge is not always reliable, because we are all susceptible to collective errors—history is filled with such examples. Even more frequently, multiple conflicting viewpoints coexist. In such cases, which perspective will AI choose to champion?

The next step is to create true intelligence, capable of understanding, and providing answers to new situations and topics. In the form of the next judicious steps derived from the various tactical patterns related to the relevant subject.

Intuition is at the base of all science, and I am convinced that, in the medium term, AIs will also be endowed with intuition. Current artificial intelligence systems, although effective in data search and analysis, lack this key capability. This lack results from the statistical nature of these models, which are unable to synthesize a new response to unprecedented situations.

Organic AI, by drawing inspiration from cerebral processes, offers a path to filling this gap. Intuition is a sort of shortcut that synthesizes the knowledge present in the brain in response to a given situation/question, in relation to the relevant tactical patterns. One must have a rich experience in a given field to be capable of good intuition in that field. However, once the uniqueness of perspective is in place, its value is priceless.

This reminds me of the well-known story of the Kouros from the Getty Museum in Los Angeles, told by Malcolm Gladwell in his book on intuition, *Blink. The Power of Thinking Without Thinking.*[6] For its inauguration, the museum, seeking an iconic masterpiece—its own *Venus de Milo*—acquired a Greek statue of seemingly perfect classical proportions. It ticked all the boxes analyzed by the different experts, and the results were consistent, perfectly compatible with a Kouros: analysis of the marble by scintigraphy, place of origin, style, age… The bundle of results from the analytical approach was convergent, the museum had broken open its piggy bank. The day of the inauguration arrives, and all the high society of art historians gather in the museum's hall. The guests discover the statue, and instantly, a coldness sets in. How could the museum's management have bought such a piece of junk?

6. Malcolm Gladwell, *Blink. The Power of Thinking Without Thinking* (Boston: Back Bay Books, 2005).

Such is intuition. No matter how many rational boxes you tick, there are certain problems for which reason does not hold the answer. I'm working in silence. Something green hops on the branch of a tree in the garden. It whistles. It's a parakeet. I need an immediate response because it could have been an imminent danger, and there's a set of shortcuts in my brain that allow me to quickly determine what it is, to make a decision, roughly the right one. Intuition works as a cognitive shortcut, allowing ultra-fast decisions based on an unconscious synthesis of all our prior experiences. This process, although immediate, results from a long accumulation of learning. And one of our big questions is how to implement these mechanisms in artificial intelligence. There seems to be a tension between the rational and the intuitive: the more we adopt an analytical and detailed approach, the more we risk losing access to intuitive processes, which rely on a global and non-conscious synthesis. It's a bit like trying to remember your dreams: the more you try, the more you focus on them, the more they escape. To operate, one must be able to synthesize.

One can have intuitions in one field, and none in others. Thus, a precise intuition in a particular field requires a long process of immersion and learning in that field.

But some fields are more or less inaccessible to intuition, or at least quite impervious to it. I love quantum mechanics, and I also find string theory fascinating, this model of a physical space with eleven dimensions, developed to attempt to unify the fundamental forces of nature, to merge quantum mechanics and gravity. For theories as complex as quantum mechanics or string theory, few can have a true intuition of them. Although the equations allow for precise calculations, the mental representation of these concepts remains beyond reach, even for the greatest minds. The equations speak to us, symbolic chains on which mathematical geniuses can have intuitions, like physicist Paul Dirac, who won the Nobel Prize in Physics along with Edwin Schrödinger in 1933. But when Dirac was asked how he arrived at one of his fundamental ideas on momentum, he said he started with the mathematics. He wanted a beautiful equation, and that mathematical beauty was for him a guarantee of truth—and his equation was experimentally proven to be correct.

An artificial intelligence, freed from biological limits, could be immersed in a virtual universe with eleven dimensions and, through repeated experiments, develop its own intuitions. By interacting in environments inaccessible to humans, it could reinvent our understanding of the laws of nature. We are already witnessing breakthroughs with AIs like those of DeepMind, which reveal mathematical and algorithmic concepts beyond our human capabilities.

This finally reminds me of the fascinating representation of AI in Spike Jonze's film *Her*, where the artificial intelligence, as it evolves, ends up transcending the human perception of time. By being simultaneously present in a multitude of interactions, it no longer perceives time as a series of linear moments. What, for us, constitutes a continuous flow of time becomes for it a landscape in which it can freely navigate, flattened by its parallel processing capacity. Just as we live on time scales many orders of magnitude faster than those of trees, a future AI could "flatten" time and evolve on scales that surpass us, perhaps coming close to the fundamental scales of time, like the "chronon," if such a unit truly exists.

Who knows what discoveries these AIs could make?

Bibliography

Reference works

Asimov, Isaac. *I, Robot. HarperVoyager,* 2013.

Berthoz, Alain. *La Simplexité*. Odile Jacob, 2009.

Burnod, Yves, and Nikki. *The Panoramic Brain: A Panorama of Brain Resources to Boost Education and Address the Web and AI Challenges*. 2024.

Cixin, Liu. *The Three-Body Problem*. Actes Sud, 2016.

Darrouzet, Éric. *Les Insectes Sociaux*. Quae, 2016.

Dehaene, Stanislas. *Learning! The Talents of the Brain, the Challenge of Machines*. Odile Jacob, 2018.

— *The Code of Consciousness*. Odile Jacob, 2014.

— *The Neurons of Reading*. Odile Jacob, 2007.

Dorigo, Marco, and Thomas Stützle. *Ant Colony Optimization*. MIT Press, 2004.

Dorigo, Marco, Éric Bonabeau, and Guy Theraulaz. *Swarm Intelligence: From Natural to Artificial Systems*. Oxford University Press, 1999.

Gladwell, Malcolm. *Intuition: The Power of Thinking without Thinking*. Back Bay Books, 2005.

Hawkins, Jeff. *1000 Brains: A New Understanding of the Brain and Artificial Intelligence*. Quanto, 2023 (2021).

Hawkins, Jeff, and Sandra Blakeslee. *On Intelligence: How a New Understanding of the Brain Will Lead to the Creation of Truly Intelligent Machines*. Times Books, 2004.

Hofstadter, Douglas, and Emmanuel Sander. *Analogy: The Core of Thought*. Odile Jacob, 2013.

Hubel, David Hunter, and Thorsten Wiesel. *Brain and Visual Perception: The Story of a 25-Year Collaboration*. Oxford University Press, 2005.

Kahneman, Daniel. *Thinking, Fast and Slow*. Flammarion, 2012 (2011).

Le Cun, Yann. *When the Machine Learns: The Revolution of Artificial Neurons and Deep Learning*. Odile Jacob, 2019.

Mountcastle, Vernon B. *The Mindful Brain: Cortical Organization and a Selective Theory of Brain Function*. MIT Press, 1978.

Seeley, Thomas D. *The Democracy of Bees*. Quae, 2017 (Princeton University Press, 2011).

Touzet, Claude. *The Responses of the Neural Theory of Cognition*. Vol. 1: *Consciousness, Intelligence, Free Will*. La Machotte, 2010.

— Vol. 2: *Hypnosis, Sleep, Placebo*. La Machotte, 2014.

Üexkull, Jacob von. *Animal and Human Environments*. Rivages, 2010.

Whorf, Benjamin Lee. *Language, Thought, and Reality*. MIT Press, 1964.

Wohlleben, Peter. *The Secret Life of Trees*. Les Arènes, 2017 (Ludwig Verlag, 2015).

Important articles

Hubel, David H., and Thorsten N. Wiesel. "Receptive Fields, Binocular Interaction and Functional Architecture in the Cat's Visual Cortex." *Journal of Physiology*, 1962.

— "Receptive Fields of Single Neurons in the Cat's Striate Cortex." *Journal of Physiology*, 1959.

Human Brain Project. "A Closer Look at Scientific Advances." *Human Brain Project*, 2023.

Leergaard, T.B., and J.G. Bjaalie. "Atlas-Based Data Integration for Mapping the Connections and Architecture of the Brain." *Science*, 2022.

Mountcastle, Vernon. "The Functional Properties of the Light-Sensitive Neurons of the Posterior Parietal Cortex Studied in Waking Monkeys: Foveal Sparing and Opponent Vector Organization." *Journal of Neuroscience*, 1981.

— "An Organizing Principle for Cerebral Function: The Unit Module and the Distributed System." 1978.

— "Modality and Topographic Properties of Single Neurons of the Cat's Somatic Sensory Cortex." *Journal of Neurophysiology*, 1957.

Tsao, Doris, et al. "The Code for Facial Identity in the Primate Brain." *Cell*, 2017.

— "Functional Compartmentalization and Viewpoint Generalization within the Macaque Face-Processing System." *Science*, 2010.

— "A Cortical Region Consisting Entirely of Face-Selective Cells." *Science*, 2006.

Communications

Le Cun, Yann. "Objective-Driven AI: Towards AI Systems That Can Learn, Remember, Reason, Plan, Have Common Sense, Yet Are Steerable and Safe." Intervention at Collège de France, 02.09.2024.

Pirim, Patrick. "Perceptive Invariance and Associative Memory Between Perception and Semantic Representation: A Universal Semantic Representation Implemented in a System on Chip (SoC)." In *Living Machines 2016*, LNAI 9793, edited by N.F. Lepora et al., 275-287. Springer International Publishing Switzerland, 2016. DOI: <10.1007/978-3-319-42417-0_25>.

Pirim, Patrick. "Generic Bio-Inspired Chip Model Based on Spatio-Temporal Histogram Computation: Application to Car Driving by Gaze-Like Control." 2013. DOI: <10.1007/978-3-642-39802-5_20>. Lepora, Nathan F., et al. "Proceedings of the Second International Conference on Biomimetic and Biohybrid Systems." Conference in London, 2013. <https://dl.acm.org/doi/proceedings/10.5555/2529563>.

Krüger, Norbert, et al. "Deep Hierarchies in the Primate Visual Cortex: What Can We Learn for Computer Vision?" *IEEE Transactions on Pattern Analysis and Machine Intelligence*. DOI: <10.1109/TPAMI.2012.272>.

Table of contents

Acknowledgements

This book marks a milestone in the development of the company AnotherBrain, following many trials, paths explored, new avenues considered and soon abandoned, simplified models, enriched, refined, then reformulated, hacked, adapted—essentially a winding path that led us to reach a high plateau in our journey toward the heights of artificial general intelligence. A high plateau, a step where we arrive with a fairly complete model of Organic AI and partial, promising accomplishments that open the way to a demonstrator. We are not yet at the summit, but we have left the dense forests behind, and the trail is clear before us. Many have contributed to our progress, and I wish to thank them.

Starting with Anne-Sophie Madoire-Rouzaud, my road companion who co-piloted the development of AnotherBrain with me and, along with Patrick Ropert, was instrumental in crystallizing the idea for this book. On the scientific side, first and foremost, of course, Patrick Pirim, whose essential contribution is outlined in the book, as well as Yves Burnod, whom I wish to thank deeply for his clear and precise thinking, which has been a beacon throughout all these years at AnotherBrain—and even before. Without you, neither this book nor probably AnotherBrain would have existed. Finally, Jeff Hawkins, whom I have never had the honor of meeting personally, but whose atypical, simplifying, and illuminating research was the spark that led me to create AnotherBrain. Thanks to you, Subutai, and your teams. Many other scientists played a significant role and are cited and thanked throughout the book.

But most of all, I wish to thank each person at AnotherBrain who, throughout these seven years since Valentine's Day 2017, has played a role in the emergence of our current model of Organic AI. Through new ideas or by clearing the paths opened by others, as well as exploring avenues that were ultimately not pursued. In no particular order: Guillaume Havard, Laurent Tourte, Marwa Hafsi, Adrien Martel, Stefano Tiso, Loubna El Gueddari, Maxellende

Julienne, Sophie Deragobian, Florent Remis, Charlotte Saglier, Jean Baptiste Le Reste, Pierre Mirouze, Magsen Chebini, Tao Li, François Denquin, Julien Goumard, Éric Mercier, Vincent Gloux, Antonella Florio, Pauline de Lavallade, Marc Sanselme, Matthieu Thiboust, Caroline Le Duigou, Julien Gosseaume, David Dehaene, Nicolas Druizard, Valentin Foucher, Julien Akir, Leslie Marande, Gladys Baudet, Guillaume Pinto.

www.ingramcontent.com/pod-product-compliance
Lightning Source LLC
LaVergne TN
LVHW022215200926
848481LV00006B/1984
9791037045140